To Be an Artist:

MUSICIANS, VISUAL ARTISTS, WRITERS, AND DANCERS SPEAK

Camille Colatosti

E L Kurdyla Publishing, LLC

Bowie, Maryland

ISBN 978-1-61751-004-5

Copyright © 2012 by Camille Colatosti

LCCN: 2011944616

The paper used in this publication meets the minimum requirements of the American National Standard for Information Sciences-Permanence of Paper for Printed Materials, ANSI Z39.48-1992.

For Dan Colatosti.

And for Karen Spang, the bravest and best person I know.

"Do the thing you think you cannot do."

—Eleanor Roosevelt

TABLE OF CONTENTS

ACKNOWLEDGEMENTS

I would like to thank Phillip Kwik for his help every step of the way. Without his support, this book, and so many other parts of my life, would not be possible.

I would also like to thank Bill Banfield, Juliana Horton, and Lori Landay for their help and advice.

Chapter 1:

Victor Wooten. Credit Steven Parke. Used with permission. All rights reserved.

Chapter 2:

Nona Hendryx. Credit Bob Gruen. Used with permission. All rights reserved.

Labelle—Pattie Labelle, Nona Hendryx. and Sarah Dash. Credit Michael Putland. Used with permission. All rights reserved.

Chapter 3:

Bill Banfield. Used with permission. All rights reserved.

Chapter 4:

Michael Bearden. Credit Carin Baer. Used with permission. All rights reserved.

Chapter 5:

The Desire of Dali's Women. Copyright Caroline Harvey. Used with permission. All rights reserved.

You Have a Voice. Copyright Caroline Harvey. Used with permission. All rights reserved.

Caroline Harvey. Credit Couron Marselle. Used with permission. All rights reserved.

Chapter 6:

Alicia Valdes-Rodriguez. Used with permission. All rights reserved.

Chapter 7:

Ellen Priest: Self-portrait Palette. Used with permission. All rights reserved.

Jazz: Edward Simon's "Venezuelan Suite" #10. Copyright Ellen Priest. Used with permission. All rights reserved.

Chapter 8:

Chapter 9:

Chapter 10:

Chapter 11:

Chapter 12:

Chapter 13:

Chapter 14:

Chapter 15:

Chapter 16:

PREFACE

I teach songwriting and poetry at Berklee College of Music in Boston. It's been a delight: to be surrounded by so many artists—some with international success, some with modest success; some with total passion and commitment to their art, some along for the ride; some with deep insight into their process, some simply surfing on the waves of intuition.

Over the years, I've been able to come to some conclusions about what art is, what it means, and what it is to commit to a life in the arts.

But it took me years.

I wish I'd been able to start it all by reading this book. It would have given me a context—a basis for listening to all the folks I've met—a platform from which to ask questions. I would have been able to bounce their answers off the kaleidoscope of perspectives you'll find inside these covers. It would have deepened my understanding of what I was doing, and why, so much earlier.

Camille Colatosti has filled these pages with the ideas and perspectives of some amazing and thoughtful artists from both inside and outside the Berklee community. I'm happy to be able to read it now, and hear echoes of those long conversations I had years ago over coffee or wine, or while just waiting for a bus.

Thanks to Camille, you now have the advantage of reading this book early in your journey through the sacred territories of the arts. Take your time and listen hard. It will provide you with landmarks that will chart your path—keep you from losing your way in the glitz and fanfare that sinks so many careers. Surrounded by all the temptations bubbling up through our current *American Idol* mentality, it is easy to be distracted by results rather than the beauty and joy available in the journey itself.

I've often marveled at the clarity and insight of Berklee's motto, "Esse quam videre" — to *be* rather than to seem to be. That is the North Star that the artists in these pages see so clearly. This book will help you recognize it too. Pay attention, and bon voyage.

Pat Pattison
Professor, Berklee College of Music
December 2011

Introduction

For Artists and All of Us

This book is for artists. By that, I mean it is for all of us.

It is for professional performing and fine artists, for writers, for art students, and aspiring artists. And it is also for anyone who loves art, who follows music, theater, and film—for anyone who has ever written a poem, painted a picture, or performed in a community choir or local theater. It is for everyone who understands and values art and its place in the world.

To Be an Artist is a conversation with today's successful and prominent artists from a variety of disciplines—musicians, visual artists, digital artists, poets, writers, activists, and scholars. All of them discuss what it means to be an artist today, how they perceive their craft and their world, and the role of art in society. They agree that artists' creativity and success come not only from intense focus on their craft, but, also, from their development of a worldview—from their wider vision and understanding of the world in which they live.

To be an artist, suggest those featured in this book, it is necessary to focus on more than one's art. Artists need space for reflection; they need to discover a way to live a life of balance; and they need to probe some of life's most enduring concerns: one's relationship with society, with nature, with faith, and with others.

To be an artist, it is necessary to understand one's own definition of success. Likewise, artists need to explore their relationships with family and with the public. Artists examine their political views, their understanding of technology, and the ways that they survive and thrive in a society that seems not to value art. They need to look at how they have developed as artists, as they consider their own understanding of fame and the impact of commercialism on art.

The artists about whom you will read discuss the need to learn as much as possible about as much as possible. This broad study, often described in a university setting as exploration of the liberal arts—the study of the humanities, history, social sciences, natural sciences, and mathematics—feeds the artist's mind, soul and heart. As performance poet, dancer, and yoga expert **Caroline Harvey** tells us in Chapter 5, when she invites all artists to experience their world as fully as possible:

"As an artist your responsibility is to live in the world and experience everything, comment on it or change it....Everything feeds into your art. There is no class that I have taken, no book that I have ever read, that does not feed into my art."

This focus beyond art, this development of a worldview beyond their profession, enables artists to improve their work, as they come to understand themselves better and come to see how their art fits into society.

All of the artists emphasize lifelong learning. They stress the importance of having an open mind and continuing to explore every day. For some of the artists included in this book—singer-songwriters **Janis Ian** and **Nona Hendryx**, for instance, who began their careers while they were in their teens—developing this worldview happened almost exclusively outside of the classroom. Yet, even they acknowledge key classroom learning experiences. Ian notes the value of her study with expert acting teacher Stella Adler, while Hendryx recalls an important high school English teacher.

Stella Adler (1901–1992) founded the Stella Adler Studio of Acting in New York City in 1949. Alumni include Marlon Brando and Robert DeNiro.

For other artists included in these pages—vocalist **Bobby McFerrin,** musician and composer **Bill Banfield,** painter **Ellen Priest**, and novelist **Alisa Valdes-Rodriguez**—their artistic journey was furthered by a college education that included not only study of their art but also broad and diverse learning.

This expansive study is less about the content of the disciplines being examined than it is about inquiry and self-realization. One studies liberal arts, one studies broadly, to explore and learn something about him or herself. "Know thyself," was Socrates' guiding principle. "To thine own self be true," says *Hamlet*'s Polonius to his son Laertes. To be a better artist—in fact, to be a better human being—one must know oneself, and that is what broad study, study in the liberal arts, helps one achieve.

Artists Speak

In this book, the artists who tell their stories speak about the ways that developing this broad worldview—thinking beyond the art form itself to consideration of art's impact and meaning in the world—is essential today. Artist after artist repeats the same message: To be an artist, to be able to create, one must understand the world and one's place in it. And this understanding comes through broad and diverse study.

In Chapter 3, musician and composer **Bill Banfield** argues that "part of being an artist is having the courage to speak powerfully, critically, and humanely about the world we live in." This takes "courage," Banfield reiterates, and it takes knowledge—knowledge of history, diverse cultures, and the natural world. It takes critical and creative thinking. It takes developing an understanding of one's self and of one's personal and social responsibility.

Nona Hendryx, in Chapter 2, emphasizes that music is about more than entertainment. Music, she says, is about life. "Music can say things that nothing else can."

Dancer and choreographer **Otis Sallid** says, in Chapter 13, that "all art is about communication and language." Great art, he continues, "is not necessarily about the thing itself. Yes, it is important to hit the notes but equally as important to awaken the spirit." He continues, "Great art is great for a reason. You want to know why. One of the biggest things that artists can do while they are studying is learn everything."

Performance poet **Bruce George,** co-founder of Def Poetry Jam on HBO, states in Chapter 11, that artists are "the guides who take people from the individual to the social. "Artists," says George, "need to understand their world" and this comes through "study and lifelong learning." It is the constant desire to know, to learn, and to inquire that facilitates and sustains an artist's career.

Today, more and more aspiring artists begin their creative journeys through study in arts colleges—like Berklee College of Music, Columbia College Chicago, the College of Visual Arts, Juilliard, the Rhode Island School of Design, and the New England Conservatory—institutions that focus exclusively on the fine and performing arts. More of today's authors are earning Bachelor and Master of Fine Arts in Writing degrees. This makes it even more important to consider the kinds of education that young artists need to enhance their success as artists and as people.

At most colleges, arts colleges, and other institutions of higher education, courses are separated into those in the major and those general education or liberal arts courses beyond the major. Most often, the latter are given a kind of lesser status, and may even be seen by students as classes "to be gotten out of the way" rather than as study that must exist in strong partnership with the major.

However, this partnership is especially important with arts study. For it is that partnership, that understanding of the relationship between arts study and broader liberal education, that is most beneficial to helping the aspiring artist develop.[1] *New York Times*-bestselling author **Doug Stanton** explains this in Chapter 12, as he states that writers shape stories and make their work meaningful by tackling and trying to solve key problems. "In education," he says, "if you can instill in a student a sense of curiosity, a sense of being comfortable with terror, then you are successful." By "terror," he explains, "I mean helping students understand how it feels to be in the middle of chaos in a fluid environment, helping them figure out how to think moment by moment…how to find meaning in what they see around them." That, he helps us understand, is the work of an artist.

While much has been written about the need for a broad worldview, for wide and diverse study in liberal arts, for those preparing for careers in business, law or medicine, there has been little discussion about the benefits of a broad education to the artist him or herself.[2]

As head of the Liberal Arts program at Berklee College of Music, a premier college of contemporary music and, with 4,000 undergraduate students, one of the largest arts colleges in the United States, I have firsthand experience of the kinds of education that young artists receive. I have also seen the very positive value of broad study—study beyond the boundaries of the arts discipline—to the developing artist. I understand what the artists in this book are saying to us: When artists allow themselves to think outside of their art—to exceed the boundaries of their own specialization—they grow as people and become better artists.

In my more than 25 years of teaching at the college level and designing liberal arts programs for students planning specialized careers, I have seen how broad and general study helps young people develop and grow stronger in their chosen fields. At Berklee, I have watched aspiring artists—initially so focused on the study of the technical aspects of their craft—grow in their understanding of themselves and their world as they study philosophy, history, literature, mathematics, foreign languages, and psychology. As a result of this growth, they become more creative, more willing and able to use rules and technical aspects of art as a place of beginning, rather than a place of ending. I have seen aspiring artists gain the confidence they need to create something new.

Purposes of College

College has two purposes: It prepares students for their professions (for careers and work) and for their life beyond work. A Charlie King folk song reminds us that "My life is more than my work, and my work is more than my job."[3] While preparing students for careers is important— and perhaps becomes more so as the cost of college tuition increases—it is really the secondary function of education.

The primary purpose of a college education is to learn about oneself, to open one's mind to new possibilities, to expand and grow, so that the whole of life—not only work but all of life's variety—can be embraced fully and successfully. This means that college, in its best sense, should not only be an *informational* experience—one that enables students to acquire new knowledge and skills—but a *transformational* experience, one that leads students to change holistically as they come to understand themselves, to reflect upon and confirm their choices, and to embark on this thing called adulthood.

Preparing for life as an artist is a huge commitment. Any artist—as is echoed in this book—will tell you that this undertaking cannot be approached lightly. It requires a dedication to a certain direction and a passion. And it is often difficult. Of course, many artists struggle to make a living. While some aspiring artists have the support of their family and friends as they embark on their journey, many do not. I cannot tell you the number of students who enroll in Berklee College of Music—after a very extensive and competitive application, audition, and interview process—against the advice of their families. Their parents may have urged students to put the guitar down and, instead, choose a "more practical" career.

As northern Michigan painter and folk artist **Greg Jaris** recounts, in Chapter 14: Even after he had completed his Master of Fine Arts degree, his father said to him, "You got your art degree now, that's fine, but what are you going to *do*?" In Chapter 8, visual and sound artist **China Blue** acknowledges that "being an artist in the United States can be hard. It is seen as a really odd thing to be doing. As an artist, you experience that nearly every day. People think it is weird. Why would you bother?"

In Chapter 16, **Janis Ian** explains that "no matter how much society thinks being famous is cool, it is also telling you, 'What do you mean, you are going to be a musician? That is no way to earn a living. Go do something else.'" To be an artist, she continues, one must persevere and be tough enough to resist the pressure because "there is something inside of you too big to get out any other way."

To foster that "something inside of you," artists need tools, education, and time. As Ian explains, "To become an artist takes a lot more than talent. To become an artist is a long slow arduous process." Yet, it is essential, because art is needed not only by the artist him or herself. It is needed by all of us. "Artists," says Ian, "hold chaos at bay. Artists are storytellers." And, "artists keep our history for us."

In this book, artist after artist shows how being able to understand the world and one's place in it makes it possible to sustain a long and successful creative career. Real artists share their life lessons, as they look at themselves not only as artists, but as varied and complex people—people who look at the world through more than one lens.

Chapter Overview

In the chapters that follow, artists' experiences are organized around key aspects of learning, beginning with a focus on self-understanding, moving on to an exploration of the relationship among the arts, progressing to an assessment of culture and community, and concluding with a reflection on the role of the artist in the world today to bring joy and to tell the truth.

Part I, Knowing Oneself: Choosing an Artist's Life, focuses on artists' gaining an understanding of themselves. Artists discuss the importance of finding oneself. They explore their personal identities and they discuss their own aesthetic sensibilities. They comment on the importance of being comfortable in one's own skin, and they note the ways that they re-defined themselves as their careers changed.

Part II, Exploring Interrelationships Among the Arts, examines how the performing and fine arts build on and sustain each other. Artists explore the relationship among writing, visual arts, music, dance, digital arts, and other types of performance.

Part III, Sustaining Culture and Community, explores the role of the artist as a member and leader of his or her community. Artists discuss the ways that their work is affected by and impacts current social issues. Likewise, artists discuss their responsibility to and interaction with the society in which they live.

Part IV, Bringing Joy; Telling the Truth, explores the ways that the arts bring joy and meaning to the world in which we live. Artists tell the truth. They help us understand the world as well as experience happiness and beauty.

Artists as Society's Eyes, Ears, and Interpreters

The understandings presented in this book are important not only to aspiring artists, but to all of us. We need artists to remain the eyes, ears, and interpreters of the very complex world in which we live. Artists more and more feel the pressure of the commercial world. Of course, artists should be able to pay their bills and should achieve commercial success. Yet, the pressure of the commercial needs to be balanced with the creative, so that the artist is not lost, so that the artist is aware of the choices he or she is making and can feel that those choices are good, ethical, and sound ones that fit into a creative context.

Helping developing artists shape and control their art, their direction and their lives, helping them prepare for life, is what this book is all about. I believe that the artist in all of us can find something here to guide our journey. Please enjoy—as you create and learn.

Notes

[1] For more about the intersection of liberal education and artists' education, see the minutes from the conferences of the Consortium for the Liberal Education of Artists, http://www.clearts.org/HOME.html. Also see the proceedings from the National Conferences on Liberal Arts and the Education of Artists, sponsored by the School of Visual Arts, http://www.schoolofvisualarts.edu/ug/index.jsp?sid0=1&sid1=46&page_id=497#proceedings.

[2] The excellent work of the American Association of Colleges and Universities provides general and comprehensive resources about the value of a liberal education to students in professional education programs, including law, medicine and business. See The American Association of Colleges and Universities. 2009. Web. 28 August 2009.

Also see The Business, Entrepreneurship and Liberal Learning (BELL) Project, sponsored by the Carnegie Foundation for the Advancement of Teaching and the Teagle Foundation. This is a 3-year project, begun in 2009, "to determine how educators can help ensure that undergraduate students who major in business and other professional fields also gain the benefits of a strong liberal arts education." For more information, see "Business, Entrepreneurship and Liberal Learning (BELL)." The Carnegie Foundation for the Advancement of Teaching. 2009. Web. 24 August 24, 2010.

Additional helpful sources include:

Berkowitz, Peter. "Liberal Education, Then and Now." *Policy Review* 140 (Dec 2006-Jan 2007): 1-9. Web. 14 July 2010.

Chew, Byron E, and Cecilia McInnis-Bowers. "Blending Liberal Art & Business Education." *Liberal Education* 90.1 (Winter 2004): 56-63. Print.

Jones, Roberts T. "Liberal Education for the 21st Century: Business Expectations." *Liberal Education* 91.2 (Spring 2005): 32-37. Print.

Hermann, Mary. "Linking Liberal and Professional Learning in Nursing Education." *Liberal Education* 90.4 (Fall 2004): 42-47. Print.

Paris, David C. *Business and the Liberal Arts: Integrating Professional and Liberal Education: Report of a Symposium on the Liberal Arts and Business, May 2007.* Washington, D.C.: Council of Independent Colleges, 2007.

Shulman, Lee. "Pedagogies of Uncertainty." *Liberal Education* 91.2 (Spring 2005): 18-25. Print.

[3] Charlie King. "Our Life is More than Our Work." *Two Good Arms.* Charlie King and Karen Brandow (charlieandkaren@charlieking.org). 1992.

PART I

Knowing Oneself: Choosing an Artist's Life

Introduction

Part I, Knowing Oneself: Choosing an Artist's Life, focuses on artists' gaining an understanding of themselves. To be an artist, one must know oneself. The artists in the section that follows explore their personal identities and the ways they developed their aesthetic sensibilities. They comment on the importance of being comfortable in one's own skin, and they note the ways that they re-defined themselves as their careers changed.

In Chapter 1, Grammy Award-winning bassist **Victor Wooten** focuses on the importance of "being good at being you." For him, everything starts not with talent, not with schooling, not with anything outside of oneself, but with the inner self, "who you are as a person."

In Chapter 2, former Labelle member **Nona Hendryx** discusses her "metamorphosis" as an artist, from singer to singer-songwriter to musician-singer-songwriter. With each development in her career, she came to understand herself. In fact, for Hendryx, her almost 50-year career is still going strong and has been possible only because she has come to understand who she is.

In Chapter 3, musician and composer **Bill Banfield** discusses personal identity and aesthetics—exploring ways that artists come to develop their own aesthetic sensibility and artistic philosophy.

In Chapter 4, musical director, keyboardist, and composer **Michael Bearden**, believes that "nobody can be you better than you can. So be yourself. Find out what that is and be that. And the good thing about art," he says, "is that whatever that is, you will be right."

In Chapter 5, **Caroline Harvey**—a performance poet, dancer, and yoga expert—links all of her artistic work to express what she sees as her authentic self. She is dedicated to helping others "heal" by assisting them in their own self-exploration. For Harvey, finding her voice and helping others find theirs is crucial to her work.

For all the artists in this section, understanding oneself is key to their work and their lives.

CHAPTER 1

Victor Wooten

Photo used with permission.

Born into a Band—Understanding Oneself

Victor Wooten is one of the most celebrated bass players of all times. A five-time Grammy Award-winning bassist, Wooten is known for his solo work and his work as a member of Béla Fleck and The Flecktones. Wooten is also a skilled naturalist and teacher, a published author, magician, husband, and father of four. His book, The Music Lesson: A Spiritual Search for Growth through Music *(Berkley/Penguin 2006), teaches us that the gifts we receive from music mirror those from life, and that every movement, phrase, and chord has its own meaning, as long as we remain open to finding it.*

Wooten has won most every major award given to a bass guitarist. He was voted Bassist of the Year by Bass Player Magazine *three times, the only person to have won the award more than once. His 1996 solo debut album,* A Show of Hands, *was voted one of the most important bass recordings of all time.*

Wooten released What Did He Say? *in 1997; the Grammy-nominated* Yin-Yang *in 1999; the double CD* Live in America *in 2001;* Soul Circus *in 2005; and* Palmystery *in 2008. With Stanley Clarke and Marcus Miller, Wooten formed the group SMV and released the album* Thunder *in 2008.*

Along with his work as a performer and recording artist, Wooten runs a Bass/Nature Camp. Founded in 1999, the camp has helped hundreds of musicians who visit the 147-acre Wooten Woods Retreat to study with Wooten and other master musicians and naturalists.

In this chapter, Wooten discusses the way art begins with understanding "who you are as a person."

While he is humbled and grateful for his numerous music industry honors, Victor Wooten works neither to please the industry nor to achieve fame. For Wooten, family and being a good and honorable person are at the center of all he does. His biggest success is, as he says, that he is "a good person in the eyes of my parents." For Wooten, this "is the biggest reward I could get, because that was the main thing they were concerned about." Wooten's assessment reveals a great deal about him. For him, success grows from a personal commitment, a sense of values, and a clear understanding of one's own relationship to one's community, one's family, and one's self.

Wooten's parents were his primary mentors and a tremendous influence on him, responsible for much that he has achieved. Part of a military family, Wooten grew up in Hawaii, later moving to the continental United States, living in California and Virginia. He is the youngest of five sons—Regi, Roy, Rudy, and Joseph—all musicians. As he explains, "My parents weren't so concerned about whether we were good musicians and whether we practiced and all that kind of stuff. Of course, once we chose that as a career, they wanted us to do that. But they were most concerned about how we were as people.

"I feel that I have succeeded at that in their eyes. That's what I am most happy about. To have them be pleased with me as a person means the world. And next after that, doing my best to be a good husband and father to my four kids. All of that means way more than any awards I could get for music and anything else.

"Most people know me for music," says Wooten. But his family, "they know me for me. I am a person first. They helped me grow up to be an honest person, a person with a good heart, and a person who is not just concerned with my own self for selfish reasons, but a person who helps others grow and shares whatever goodness I have or receive. I hopefully will use that to help other people become better and reach their goals." Wooten never forgets this and does not let his commercial success affect his inner sense of personhood.

Being Good at Being You

For Wooten, everything starts not with talent, not with schooling, not with anything outside of oneself, but with the inner self, with "who you are as a person. To become really good at anything else, it makes the most sense to be good at being you. Being good at being you means being truthful to yourself and truthful to who you are in every instance that you can, not having to be someone else. That is what is going to help you be successful at anything else because you are already successful at your core."

Wooten continues, "My mom used to tell us five brothers when we were young and playing music, 'You boys are already successful. The rest of the world just doesn't know it yet.'"

He admits that he didn't understand this philosophy as a child, but now, being a parent, he realizes the "profoundness" of these ideas. His mother's belief in Wooten and his brothers being good and true to themselves, her decision not to pressure them to achieve external success but to define success internally, helped him and his brothers see "that we did not have to become anything greater than what we were. We were already great. We were already successful. We were already there. All we had to do was keep doing what we were doing. In doing that, we would become better. We would learn more about our life's work, and other people would start to take notice."

And, says Wooten, "That is exactly what happened."

Family

Wooten explains that his life story might be more interesting, might make for a better movie, if he could point to a time of hardship and recovery, a time when he doubted himself, was all alone in the world, and found success despite this. "If I could say, 'Yeah, there was one point I was down and out,' but, really, no," he admits.

"I am the youngest of five. I had four older brothers and two parents, so it is sort of like I had six parents. By the time I came along, everybody was raising me. And as much as I wanted to please my parents, I wanted to please my brothers, too.

"If I did something wrong, I would get in trouble with my parents. But then, having to face my brothers was tough. They wouldn't really say much, except, 'Man, I can't believe you did that.' And any little kid looks up to his older siblings. To disappoint my brothers was a big deal.

"And," he adds, "it's not like they had to keep me in line. It's just that I had good ideals to follow and that is what I was made out of. I was raised with it.

"I had a family. I know for a lot of people who don't have a family, they have to go out and join another one in some kind of fashion, whether it's a fraternity or a gang. I didn't need any of that because I had a strong family."

For Wooten, working with other musicians is almost like joining a new family. He approaches those with whom he plays with a sense of integrity, keeping strong his sense of himself and his commitments regarding how to relate to other people, something he learned as a son and a brother, and as a musician.

His first band, beginning at age two, involved playing with his brothers. As he grew, he also matured as a musician, relating to all his family not only as the youngest brother but also as the bass player in the band. Being a musician has always been deeply connected to his sense of personhood.

Wooten recalls the first time he began playing with musicians who were not his brothers. "In 1981, when I was 16 years old, I got a job working at an amusement park, playing in a bluegrass country band. That was my first time playing with other musicians on a day-to-day basis. I had to learn how to play with them. It was almost like joining another family, having to learn how everybody thinks. It was kind of a shock to me. But it caused me to grow as a musician."

This growth continued when Wooten moved to Nashville and began working there.

"At the end of 1988, I was the first of my brothers to move to Nashville. It was my first time living outside of my home, living away from my parents. I faced renting a place with friends and living on my own, having to make my own money. That was a challenge. But I can't say that it was real difficult. It was just that I had to do it by myself. I had been brought up in a way that allowed me to persevere."

From his core as a son, brother, and musician, he came to re-define himself as a person living away from his family. In doing so, he developed a new understanding of himself. This period of growth helped him re-affirm that music is intrinsically connected to his sense of identity.

Learning through Listening

When Wooten started playing with the amusement park band, he had to learn to listen. "Having played with my brothers, things were automatic. We knew each other so well. I knew that, okay, if I do this, he'll do that. If he does this, I should do that.

"Some of those rules changed with other musicians. It was the start of a process of turning me into a complete musician, learning to play with these other musicians. One of the biggest things I learned was listening. I learned to play less and listen more.

"Listening to the other musicians helped me know more about how to respond musically." He compares his experience of moving from one group of musicians to another to that of moving "up north from down south." "It's the same language but a different dialect. And you don't learn that dialect by talking, you learn by listening. And if you listen, you will start speaking that language or that dialect without even trying. You won't even know you're doing it until you go back south, and people will say to you, 'Wow, you've got an accent.'"

With his brothers, Wooten had learned how to play improvised music. He would "play as I wanted, and I knew that the next time I played, it was going to be different.

"Now, in the park, all of a sudden, I had to play six to eight shows a day and they had to be exactly the same. I was either going to go crazy or learn something. And I chose to learn. I learned a whole lot. I learned through listening. I felt that I was a pretty good listener already but I became much better when I started playing with other musicians."

Wooten credits trumpet player Wayne Jackson with teaching him an important lesson about listening. "I was doing a recording with Wayne. When we were in the studio, he said to me, 'Victor, remember, you have two ears. One of them is for you. The other one is for the rest of the band.' Now that was his gentle and kind way of telling me that I wasn't listening well enough."

Wayne Jackson (1941-), of the Memphis Horns, has played on more than 50 hit records, including Otis Redding's "(Sittin' on) The Dock of the Bay."

Wooten describes an exercise that challenges musicians to listen: "I will have a band play a song and I will stop them midstream. Then I may ask the guitar player what the keyboard player was playing. I may ask the drummer what was the guitar player strumming. I may ask the bass player what were the lyrics that the vocalist was singing. More times than not, no one can answer the question. But when I do this a second time, people can answer because they were listening."

Music and Identity—Being Oneself

For Wooten, art embodies the artist. His music is another representation of who he is. "It is a musical representation. When people hear my music, they are hearing different facets, different parts of me.

"When I am writing music, I am playing or saying what I feel in some way," he explains. "I think the same about any kind of art, whether it is Michael Jordan playing basketball in his artistic way. You can learn a whole lot about him when you study his game. Looking at my music or reading my book, you can learn a whole lot about me. My art form is just another version of me."

That said, Wooten is not so interested in people learning about *him*. "My main goal," he says, "is for people to learn about themselves." By showing them his "version of me," he wants to help them "reach a clear version of who they are.

"In life, one of our main problems is that we are all trying to be someone else, because we think we have to be, to please other people. But the easiest thing to be is ourselves and realize that is a great person to be. What the world needs is the best version of you possible." For Wooten, if he "could offer anybody anything, it would be helping people find themselves. I am hoping that through my music, through my artistry, other people will feel allowed to offer themselves to the rest of the world, in whatever way that is, but in an honest way."

Playing Music—Not an Instrument

"I was born into a band," explains Wooten.

"My brothers realized when I was born that if we had a bass player, we'd have a complete band. So that became me. My brothers would set up to play or practice, and there would be an empty stool with a plastic toy guitar sitting on it. I knew it was for me. So I would pick it up and strum along, as if I were playing air guitar but strumming an instrument. I was learning music before I could play a note. I didn't start playing notes. I didn't start learning an instrument. I started learning music."

This distinction is key for Wooten. "Most people learn to play an instrument. It takes a lot of time to stop playing the instrument and start playing music. The instrument remains a barrier that we have to break beyond.

"Most people don't want to hear the instrument," says Wooten. "Some musicians do. But the general public wants to hear music." He asks instrumentalists to "forget that you are even playing. Just envision a drummer. Hear that drummer. Feel the floor vibrate. Hear the cymbals. I want you to create completely that drummer in your head. After that, play along, but put zero attention on what you're playing." He tells the instrumentalist, "I want you to play along with the drummer and put 100 percent of your attention on the drummer."

Adds Wooten, "I guarantee you will hear a change when this happens. All of a sudden the bass player plays less. He or she usually plays softer. The notes sound more full. They sound rounder. It's because they're playing music with someone, not just playing an instrument by themselves. And when people play music, they always play the instrument better. This allows the listeners to hear the full band."

Continues Wooten, "If you've been playing your instrument for at least a year, it is time to stop thinking about it and to start thinking about music. Almost 100 percent of the time, you will play that instrument better."

The Language of Music

Born into a band, Wooten not only learned to play music before he learned to play the bass. As he explains, he "learned the language of music before I ever learned how to say a word. As a kid playing music, I just jammed with my brothers for years and years. The instrument wasn't that important. When I was around three or so, my brother took two strings off of one of his real guitars, wrapped it around my toy guitar, and started teaching me. *That* was my first bass. He started teaching me where to place my fingers to produce a desired tone. And so I actually started learning how to play notes on an instrument.

"But the difference here is like a kid learning to say the word 'no.' They learn to say the word 'no' really quickly because they have a need for it. In learning to play notes, I was learning songs I already knew. I was learning songs I had been playing already and, believe it or not, at that early age, I had already learned to play music in the same way a child understands the language before he learns to speak it."

To Wooten, "music is a language. Yet, the way we learn to speak English as a language and the way most people learn to speak music as a language are almost opposites of each other. As children, we learned to speak English because everyone around us was speaking it. We were allowed to speak with adults. No one told us that we were 'just a beginner.' We weren't put in a beginning class, only allowed to speak with other beginners like we do in music.

"When we messed up as small children, if we said something wrong, no one corrected us. We were allowed to say 'pus-ghetti,' for instance, instead of 'spaghetti.' It was okay. We didn't even know we were wrong. And more so, our parents started saying it wrong with us. They would say 'pus-ghetti.'

"Not only were we not made to feel wrong, we didn't know we were wrong and we were made to feel good about everything we said. We were able to maintain our freedom, when we were speaking as toddlers."

> Curtis Lee Mayfield (1942–1999) was an American soul, funk, and R&B singer, whose hits included "Freddie's Dead' and "Superfly."

The freedom and affirmation that children experience when learning to speak for the first time is a model that Wooten would like to duplicate in music instruction. He believes that the over-emphasis placed on learning notes and scales can actually inhibit students' learning of and love for music and may restrict people's musical development.

As Wooten explains, "Our beginning music students are put in a class where they are made to practice. We were never made to practice English. And so it makes me wonder how we got so good so quickly. At two years old, we could improvise with the language. We could talk with the best. We could communicate with professionals"—adults who were proficient English language speakers.

"With music, we are made to practice. We're told what we have to play and what we are not supposed to play. We're taught the right and the wrong way. And doing it the wrong way makes us feel bad. Even practicing the right way, we do it hesitantly and with our guard up because we are *afraid* of doing it the wrong way. We don't develop a musical freedom from the onset.

"Before we started taking music lessons, we were free because we played an air guitar and we did it happily with a smile on our face. There were no such things as right or wrong notes. There was only emotion and feeling. And as soon as we took music lessons, other emotions came. They were doubt, fear."

Because Wooten learned to play as a child with his brothers, he did not doubt himself. He was "playing" music with his older brothers, jamming on his toy guitar. When he switched to a real guitar, the transition was natural. He was not told the right or wrong way to play. He was not robbed of the emotion and feeling for music in order to focus on correctness. This is the way he would like to see music taught and learned.

His parents also recognized the talent of their children. "By the time I was around five," says Wooten, "my parents realized, 'Wow, these boys can play.' So they started booking gigs for us. When I was around the age of five or six, after we had moved to California, we were seen by a promoter and we started opening for big concerts." In fact, when Wooten was just six years old, the Wooten Brothers Band became the opening act for the great soul singer Curtis Mayfield.

"Basically," says Wooten, "we just never looked back. That's all I've done my whole life."

No Wrong Notes

Wooten hopes to help other musicians find what his parents nurtured in him as a child—that in playing music, one does not need to fear making mistakes.

"Most musicians are really afraid of playing wrong. And, really, all 'wrong' means to a musician is hitting the wrong notes. When I am working with people," says Wooten, "one of the first things I do is tell them there is nothing to be afraid of. We are all going to hit wrong notes for the rest of our lives. And a wrong note just means that it is not the note you meant to hit. It doesn't mean that it sounds bad. And so there are ways of making the note you did hit sound good even though you didn't mean to hit it.

"You can get to where there are no wrong notes by looking for the wrong notes. 'Okay, we're in this key,' you say to yourself, 'what are the wrong notes? What are the ones we don't want to hit?' And then, search out those notes. There are only five of them out of the twelve. There are always seven right notes in a given key, so even if I guess which notes to hit, I am going to be right more than half the time. That relieves some of the pressure right away. And if I happen to hit one of these wrong notes, what's wrong with it, what do we do?"

Wooten asks musicians to search for those wrong notes and play only those. "Normally," he says, "we hide from those notes. We hit one, we get off of it really quickly. But I tell musicians, 'That's all we're going to play. We are going to really look at these notes, and I can show you a couple of ways of making those wrong notes sound really good.'

"Once you realize how easy it is, it becomes fun, and once you make those wrong notes disappear, now instead of only having seven notes to choose from in a key, you have all twelve. So in a sense, you become free. You say, 'Wait a minute. I can play any note at any time?' Of course you can. It is all in how you play them."

Wooten continues, "Once we erase the wrong notes, we can get into what music really is—which is not just a series of notes. It's a feeling. It's an emotion, the same way language is not just a collection of words. I can't just give you a dictionary and expect you to speak clearly. There is a whole lot more to it. Once we erase the wrong notes and make you fearless of hitting one, now we can really get somewhere."

Wooten aims to "fill in" what he thinks are "holes" in the way music is taught.

"There is not a book out there on playing space in music, for instance," he says. "How do you not play? When should I not play? What does space do to the listener? If you want someone really to lean in and listen to you, the combination of dynamics and space is key. If you get really quiet, or, even better yet, stop playing, the whole room will shut up. Done in the right way—in the same way that there's different ways of using notes, there's different ways of using space, there's different dimensions of space—this can be powerful. You can turn silence up and down the same way you can turn a note up and down.

"The same is true for rhythm, how you use rhythm, what rhythms make people dance, what rhythms don't. How do you use tone? Every bass guitar and every lead guitar has a tone knob that changes our tone, but we don't really know what it does. What tone makes people dance? What tone makes people sing?"

Wooten asks people to think deeply about music. "What does music mean to you? Give me a word. People always say words like 'love,' 'happiness,' or 'fulfilling.' Beautiful words. But I never hear anybody say, 'Oh, music is scales.' 'Music is notes.' 'Music is techniques.' 'Music is theory.' Most of the people that I deal with play bass or guitar. Yet, I never ever hear anyone say 'music is a bass.'

"So, if none of those things are music, then I wonder why it is that we think about those things when it's time to play. If music is love, happiness, and fulfilling, then this should be at the forefront of our attention every time we play or listen. If it is, then you will have an audience that listens, too."

CHAPTER 2

Nona Hendryx

Photo used with permission.

Art as Metamorphosis—Remaking Herself

Nona Hendryx is a vocalist, producer, songwriter, author, and actor.

Her career began with Patti Labelle and the Bluebelles, known as the sweethearts of the Apollo Theater. She continued with the group as it changed to Labelle, a trio with Patti Labelle and Sarah Dash.

Labelle transformed from girl group to rock and roll, opening for The Who and The Rolling Stones. In 1974, the group hit gold with the song "Lady Marmalade." The national tour that followed started with a performance at the Metropolitan Opera House, where Labelle became the first contemporary pop group and the first African-American group to perform there. In 1975, the trio became the first African-American vocal group to be featured on the cover of Rolling Stone *magazine. In 1999, Labelle won an R&B Foundation Lifetime Achievement Award.*

Hendryx has also had a successful solo career, releasing her first self-titled album in 1977. She later toured with the Talking Heads, and in the 1980s, she founded her own progressive art-rock band called Zero Cool. In 1985, she wrote and recorded "Rock This House" with Keith Richards. Her 1987 recording "Why Should I Cry?" was a top five R&B hit.

Recently, Hendryx toured festivals in Europe with the Daughters of Soul—Sandra St. Victor, Indira Khan, Simone, Lalah Hathaway, and Joyce Kennedy. She also toured in the U.S with Cyndi Lauper, and reunited with Patti Labelle and Sarah Dash for a 2008-2009 tour.

Hendryx has authored a children's book called The Brownies, *and the rock opera* SkinDiver, *which she co-wrote with Charles Randolph-Wright.*

In this chapter, Hendryx discusses her "metamorphosis" as an artist and how she has come to understand who she is by being open to and embracing change.

Nona Hendryx has been performing for almost 50 years.

Her career began when she was a teen, singing with Patti Labelle and the Bluebelles. She remembers that she had "gone from being this kid, going home after school to watch *American Bandstand*, to being on *American Bandstand*. I was probably shell shocked for the first six to nine months of my being in show business," she says.

A highlight of her career came in those early days, "performing at the Apollo Theater as a teenager with people whom I had been watching. It was a thrill being on stage with people like Dinah Washington and Brook Benton—icons of rhythm and blues. My mouth was probably open for the first

Dinah Washington (1924-1963) was a blues, R&B, and jazz singer, with such hits as "Unforgettable" and "What a Difference a Day Makes."

American Bandstand (1952-1989), hosted by Dick Clark since 1957, was a show for young viewers that showcased pop, rock, and R&B music acts.

The Apollo Theater, in Harlem, New York, is one of the most prestigious entertainment venues, especially for African-American performers.

Brook Benton (1931–1988) was an R&B and pop singer and songwriter, whose more than fifty chart hits included "Rainy Night in Georgia."

few days that we performed with them. It was a school for me, watching and working with people like that." The Bluebelles' first album, *Sweethearts of the Apollo*, was recorded live at the Apollo Theater.

Since that time, her career, her art, has gone through what she calls a metamorphosis. "At one time, at that early time I felt that I was a singer," she recalls. "Then I felt that I was a singer-songwriter. And then I eventually developed into being a musician-singer-songwriter." With each metamorphosis, she has needed to deal with and adapt to changes. And, while some of these changes were difficult, she believes she is a better, stronger, and more socially aware artist because of them. The changes have helped her understand that music is not only for entertainment but also for sharing important messages and spreading good in the world.

She explains her growth: "For a long time, I listened just to the voice. All I heard was voice. I was so voice identified. That is how I heard music. This allowed me to grow with it but it was also limiting. Then, as I matured, I was able to hear all the musical parts. Now that I have known many bassists and guitar players over time, I understand why each picks the instrument he or she picks. It speaks to them. It is a way for them to have a voice. It has a lot to do with their character. The same is true for drummers.

"For me," she continues, "becoming a musician-singer-songwriter is about feeling music. Looking at music, I look from the griots and town criers through the Renaissance period to contemporary music or jazz.

A griot is a West African poet, praise singer, wandering musician, and culture keeper, whose sharing is entirely through the oral tradition.

"My goal is to be able to take music and share it with other people, whether it is one-on-one, whether it is in a club, whether it is in a huge stadium. I want to transfer what it is that inspired me to write that piece of music to someone else."

For Hendryx, "music is necessary. It is about life. How could we live if music didn't exist. Could the human race go on without music or without art? Music is needed. Music can say things that nothing else can. All instruments are brilliant. When I see music, I see it as the voice of the soul of mankind.

"I strive to continue to grow and explore music," she says, "and to use it as a healing force in the world for good."

In her own songwriting, she explains, "I can write a love song but I tend to write much more about social issues, political issues, spiritual development in terms of the self and how you evolve as a person, rather than mundane, day-to-day pedestrian type of things. The mundane is not what sustains us. Yes, we have to have sleep and food and things like that. But what really sustains us is our spirit. And not some religious gospel thing but the spirit of the human being. That is what I am always interested in."

Entering Musical Theater

Hendryx, whose career has evolved from the girl group of the 1960s to rock and roll, rhythm and blues, and funk, is now in what she describes as a new and "very creative space, working in many different genres of music and collaborating, which is something I really enjoy doing."

She began working with director, screenwriter, and producer Charles Randolph-Wright, whose credits included writing the play *Blue* and directing the 75th anniversary tour of *Porgy and Bess*. "I was not interested in doing theater before. Music for me was rock and roll, funk, not musicals," explains Hendryx. "But Charles reeled me in with several different projects. He had me writing music for him and it kept evolving. I wrote music for what he called a 'play with music.' This allowed me to say yes because, it wasn't a musical and I didn't have to do the underscore. Then we did another play together that had a string quartet. He said, 'Well, you've never written for a string quartet.' And I wanted to try that."

This developed into the play *SkinDiver*, Hendryx's original play with music. "I was starting to work on the third part of a three-part concert album when Charles said, 'This should really be on stage. I want to talk with you about it.' He told me that I should be in it, that I should

Charles Randolph-Wright (1956-) is an American performer, writer, producer, and director, whose play *Blue* features music by Nona Hendryx

Porgy and Bess is an American opera by George Gershwin, Ira Gershwin, and DuBose Heyward, whose 1935 opening featured an African-American cast.

act. We started it that way. Then I realized that I wasn't an actress and so I took myself out."

Hendryx and Randolph-Wright have been working on this project for more than seven years, because, says Hendryx, "It takes forever to do a musical." Selections were performed at Arena Stage in Washington, D.C., in spring 2010. A staged reading was performed by students at Berklee College of Music in fall 2010.

Says Hendryx, "The experience has been great. It is another part of my metamorphosis. It is so different from the rock and roll and girl group worlds that I come from. It has been great, because I have had to use other musical muscles. I have had to go back and learn things, educate myself.

What is a musical? What makes a musical work in terms of the balance of dialogue and music?

"I have had to change my ears, because musical theater singers are very different from pop, rock and roll, and rhythm and blues singers. It is a trained kind of singing. I have a great respect for people who sing in musicals and on Broadway. To do that every night, if you are the lead, eight shows a week—it is not easy. People from my world—from rock and pop—would die after a few shows."

Music Found Me

Reflecting back on the musical path she has taken, Hendryx remarks that she "is always quite amazed if I stop and think about where I came from and look at where I am. It was not my intention to be in music. It wasn't anywhere in my realm of thinking. I was going to go to college to teach history.

"Then someone asked me to sing in a group after school and I said, 'yes,' because I thought it would be fun. Now almost 50 years later, I sit here talking about those years. The musical changes that I have seen from 1960's girl group to the British invasion, moving to England, performing with the Rolling Stones, having success with Labelle for 17 years, going solo, working with the Talking Heads, Peter Gabriel, different people—it has not been something that I sought. But I believe it is where I should be."

The British Invasion was a movement of the 1960s, in which music acts from England, most notably The Beatles, became popular in the U.S.

Talking Heads was an American band, led by David Byrne, whose music combined elements of punk, rock, avant-garde, pop, and funk.

Peter Gabriel (1950-) is a British singer, musician, and songwriter, whose hits include "Shock the Monkey" and "Sledgehammer."

When people ask Hendryx how she did it, she tells them that she was not trying to find fame, enter show business, or even become a working musician. "I say: I wasn't trying to do it. It did me. It found me."

She adds, "Music will find you, too, if it is your passion and you have to do it. Art will find you, if you want it to. Whether you're a professional, semi-professional, not professional, superstar, unheard of—if you have to do this, then do it.

"If you are coming to it for other reasons, to make money, to be famous, to be in some sort of social strata, then I don't know whether it is the right place for you. You may gain all those things but it will never satisfy you in life.

"But if art finds you, you will be satisfied, no matter what happens."

Hendryx believes it is important to "keep it real," to see music as a calling and not to get an inflated sense of oneself. "I was still living at home when I first began in the business," she explains, "so it was hard for me to get a swelled head. At home, I am one of seven and my sisters and brothers, they thought it was great but I didn't get an extra piece of chicken just because I was on TV. I was still me. My mother had reservations about the music business. She thought I was meant to go to school and be a school teacher."

Hendryx adds, "You know, when you're young, you just show up and you're in awe, but you don't know that you are going to do this for the rest of your life." At the time that she began with *American Bandstand*, Hendryx did not realize that she was making a decision to enter the music industry in a permanent way.

"I think that it was the songwriting and the musical creativity that has kept me loving it and doing it," she says. "Without discovering that I could create music and that I really had a great passion for doing that, I don't think I would still be sitting here."

She continues, "Being a singer is not enough for me because it wasn't what I wanted to be. When I talk with Patti Labelle, she will say, 'I have to sing. I don't know what I would do if I didn't sing.' But I don't have to sing. I love it. I enjoy it. But what I have to do is create. That is the difference between singers and songwriters." This discovery was part of Hendryx' metamorphosis as an artist.

Teachers

Hendryx credits two people who helped her artistic development, who showed her that she could sing and write music—that she could create in a variety of ways. Hendryx recalls, "My high school English teacher, Mrs. Dinkins, who was the mother of the eventual mayor of New York City, Mayor David Dinkins,[1] was the person who introduced me to poetry and theater. She was very much responsible for helping to guide me. She got me interested in being on the stage but she also recognized my affinity for poetry. If she hadn't, I am not sure I would be here today." Mrs. Dinkins nurtured in Hendryx a love of Shakespeare and an appreciation for poetry.

The other person Hendryx sees as instrumental in her development was musician Curtis Mayfield. "He encouraged me to write my first song," says Hendryx. "We were performing in the theater and between shows, you sit around and you eat and you talk, you go to different people's dressing rooms. I was talking to Curtis about this song I had written. I didn't know what to do, how to do something. Then he said, 'Here, let me help you. A bridge might be a good idea.' That is how I wrote my first song. To have somebody like Curtis Mayfield say it was a good song and to help me on it, I was like, 'Oh, wow.'"

Her Creative Process

For Hendryx, that first song led to many, many others. She became the primary songwriter for Labelle. Since those early years, she says, "I have tried—or the muse makes me try—to create in all the ways that it's possible. But really, something has to move me, something has to inspire me."

She explains that the inspiration may be the requirement of a show on which she is working. "Someone may say to me, we need a song for this or we need a song for that, and I can go and do it because there is an inspiration there—somebody needs a particular kind of song.

"Usually," she continues, "something strikes me. And it starts building inside me. For me, it is a melody and a lyric. Eighty-five percent of the time, they come at the same time. They form in my head, and then I write something down.

"Then I go sit down at a piano or guitar and begin to flesh out the chords and really find out what the melody is. From there, if it is something that gives me the feeling of 'Yes, this needs to go on, this needs to have a life,' then I begin to start arranging it. I use the computer to do a demo for a song. Or if there is a part that I can't play, then I will get together with my guitarist or I will call up a bass player. Whatever I need, I will get someone to come and add that to it.

"Then I go into the studio. And I work with singers and give them their parts or I do the parts myself. It varies. But the beginning is that something is turned on inside of me that says, 'Hey, get me out of here. Let me out. I need to be out in the world.'" She laughs. "That's what happens."

For Hendryx, her creativity has a deep connection with her identity and with the social issues that speak to her. "I can't separate myself from social issues, political issues, gender issues, because music does not exist in a vacuum. We can say things in music that, if I stood up on a soap box and said them, people would throw tomatoes at me. But if I get up and sing them, then people will listen and maybe agree.

"Music is a powerful tool to motivate people. In music, you can go right to the heart of a person. Several words wrapped in certain notes can quell something and bring it down, so that people can listen and hear. With music, you can push right over a cliff a thing that needs to be pushed over a cliff. Hopefully, you can do that in a constructive way rather than a destructive way. Music is part of life—it is not separate from life."

Hendryx explains that sometimes political or social issues lead her to create songs with specific messages or meaning. About one song that she wrote, "Winds of Change (Mandela to Mandela)," she explains, "I wrote this in the 1980s, after reading *Part of My Soul Went with Him*,[2] which was a book ghostwritten for Winnie Mandela, because she was so under pressure from the government at the time that Nelson Mandela was arrested.

Photo used with permission.

"It is a little thin book but it just had such an effect on me. I read it when Nelson was in prison. After reading it, I sat down and wrote 'Winds of

Nelson Mandela (1918-) spent 27 years as a political prisoner in South Africa. He led the movement to end apartheid and served as president of South Africa from 1994 to 1999.

Change' in maybe 25 minutes. It is really a love song from me to her, and from her to him. That's what I mean when I say I can't separate music from social issues or from me. That song—it's a political issue, it's a social issue, it's a cultural issue. But it's wrapped in music.

"I have been performing it for a long time, and it still has the same effect on people. That is also something about music: Songs that were written 100 years ago can be performed or arranged by people today and have the same effect on people."

Hendryx has also been an outspoken activist for gay rights. In 2001, she discussed her bisexuality in *The Advocate* magazine. In 2008, she joined Cyndi Lauper on the True Colors tour, an annual music tour that benefits the Human Rights Campaign and other organizations that provide support to the LGBT community.

Successes from Change

The Advocate is an American magazine that focuses on issues important to the gay, lesbian, bisexual, and transgender community.

Cyndi Lauper (1953-) is an American pop singer whose hits include "Girls Just Want to Have Fun" and "Time after Time."

Hendryx notes the impact that change has had on her career. Events and circumstances that seemed, at first, like failures, actually led to new opportunities and helped her grow as an artist.

One change occurred early in her career, when she was singing with Patti Labelle and the Bluebelles. "At one point," she says, "we were a group of four"—Hendryx, Labelle, Sarah Dash, and Cindy Birdsong. In 1967, when Birdsong left the Bluebelles to join the Supremes, "it was a big change for us. We had always been four—one singing lead and the rest of us singing three parts in the background.

"At first, it looked like a disaster," says Hendryx. "But it was really an opportunity. If there had been four, we probably would have continued on the path we were on and that might have limited us. But because we became three, we decided to change, to become a trio and not to add a fourth. We went on to be Labelle. I don't think we would have been able to be Labelle if there had been four people. So that was a failure but not a failure at the same time. It turned out to lead to great success."

Another big change came for Hendryx when Labelle split as a group.

"We were like one person. It was hard but for me it was the best thing that could have happened. I had always had these two other pillars to lean against. Then they were gone, and I had to stand on my own and find out what music was to me, what being in show business was to me. I had to go from being part of a group to being on my own."

She reflects, "It was interesting, going from the Bluebells, a group with a lead singer with three background singers, and then becoming Labelle, with really three lead singers with one being prominent, to being on my own. In retrospect, it was probably a very gentle way to break out on my own, though it felt rough each time. It felt like life was saying, 'Okay, move here, then here, then here.' I couldn't have said that is what I should do, but that is what happened." As a result, Hendryx grew to be a solo performer, to develop as a songwriter and a musician.

She points to one other seeming disaster that shifted her career again. "I was opening for David Bowie in Europe on a major tour and all of my equipment—two trucks' full—was stolen.

"I had not been sure that I should have gone with Bowie, but I decided to do it because I had gotten all this feedback from fans. They wanted me to do it. But this was against my gut saying, 'No, it's not the right time. Don't do it.' So I went and all my equipment was stolen."

Hendryx took this as a sign that the universe was telling her that she should not have gone on that tour, that something else was waiting for her.

> David Bowie (1947-) is a British musician, whose hit singles include "Changes," "Let's Dance," and "Fame," co-written with John Lennon.

"I went home to lick my wounds. And it became an opportunity to write *SkinDiver*," an important album for Hendryx and the inspiration for her rock opera by the same name.

Says Hendryx, "I learned that, in the face of these kinds of things, music never leaves or lets you down. Things can come and go, and people can come and go. I have learned that you can be at the top of the heap, as the song says, and then you can go to the opposite of that, or you can be someplace in between.

"It is really about who I am in the world and not what I have, nor who I know, nor where I've been. That stuff is all transient. But music is always there, always with you and never lets you down."

Notes

[1] David Dinkins was the Mayor of New York City from 1990 through 1993, and is to date the only African American to hold that office.

[2] Winnie Mandela, Mary Benson, and Anne Benjamin, *Part of My Soul Went with Him*, NY: W.W. Norton, 1985. Print.

CHAPTER 3

William C. Banfield

Photo used with permission.

Personal Aesthetics

William (Bill) Banfield is a professor of Africana Studies/Music and Society at Berklee College of Music, where he directs Africana Studies programming. A native Detroiter, he earned a Bachelor of Music degree from the New England Conservatory, a Master of Theological Studies from Boston University, and a Doctorate of Musical Arts from the University of Michigan.

Banfield is a composer, whose works have been commissioned, performed, and recorded by the National, Atlanta, Dallas, Detroit, New York Virtuoso, Grand Rapids, Akron, Richmond, Toledo, Savannah, Indianapolis, Sacramento. and San Diego symphonies. He is also a performing jazz and popular music artist. His recordings can be found on Atlantic, TelArc, Collins, Centaur, Albany/Visionary, and Innova labels.

He is the author of Musical Landscapes in Color: Conversations with Black American Composers *(Scarecrow Press, 2002);* Black Notes: Essays of a Musician Writing in a Post-Album Age *(Scarecrow Press, 2004): and* Cultural Codes: Makings of a Black Music Philosophy *(Scarecrow Press, 2010).*

Banfield also works with the Quincy Jones Music Consortium, whose goal is to create a national curriculum of America's musical heritage. It is intended to explore all of the country's musical traditions and also examine how music has influenced our culture.

In this chapter, Banfield explores personal identity and aesthetics, as well as the ways that artists develop their individual sensibilities.

Sitting in his home office, surrounded by books on philosophy and aesthetics, Bill Banfield strums his signature blue guitar, as he considers how to define his own personal aesthetics. Why does he believe it is so important for developing artists to come to understand their own philosophy of art and beauty? As Banfield sees it, successful artists have a clear understanding of themselves, their identities, and their values. They also understand that the sense of self is continuously evolving.

A successful artist is not simply one who has achieved wealth or fame. "That is not it," says Banfield. "That's nice." He laughs. "But that is not what I am talking about."

Successful artists are "comfortable in their own skin." They understand that creating art is their true calling. They are always developing their craft and have made a commitment to their art. They understand that they are part of a community and have the courage to declare to the world, no matter the opposition, that they are, indeed, artists. These "Cs"—craft, commitment, community, and courage—are crucial to the artist of today.

Banfield explains, "Craft we understand. A carpenter, as a craftsperson, knows what nail to use to put that 2x4 in that wall, what hammer to use—that is part of her craft. As an artist, know your tool box.

William Edward Burghardt (W.E.B.) Dubois (1868-1963) was one of 20th century America's foremost African-American leaders, intellectuals, and spokespeople. He was a sociologist, historian, poet, and novelist.

"Commitment is about believing in what you do. If you are a dancer choreographing a piece, you have to be committed to that to the end. You need persistence to follow through, even when the work is challenging or when you face opposition.

"Community is about the other artists you work with to support your art. If you are in a big band, that is all about community. You have to support the band, support the soloist. So when you see a band on stage, whether it is the Rolling Stones or Nirvana or Duke Ellington, that is all about community. The importance of the band for community cannot be underestimated.

"But courage is most important. All these artists and thinkers—W.E.B. Dubois, Zora Neale Hurston, Andy Warhol, Madonna—courage, courage, courage. This thing about courage is such an important issue for artists, because they are frightened as young people and they don't realize that art can really break through."

Zora Neale Hurston (1891-1960), was a leading figure of the Harlem Renaissance, whose most famous novel is *Their Eyes Were Watching God* (1937).

Andy Warhol (1928-1987), a leading figure in the Pop Art movement, declared, "In the future, everyone will be world-famous for 15 minutes."

Madonna (1958-), born Madonna Louise Ciccone, is the best-selling female recording artist in the world, with more than 300 million records sold.

Society—the pressure to get a "real" job—"strangles," says Banfield. The music and commercial art industry "strangles. Parents strangle. Finances strangle—unless aspiring artists have the courage to step out there. One thing we say in religious circles, faith is the evidence of things not seen and the substance of things hoped for. You have to have faith. This is an incredibly powerful thing. That piece of faith is about courage. Part of being an artist is having the courage to speak powerfully, critically, and humanely about the world that we live in. That takes courage."

Banfield refers to theologian and philosopher Paul Tillich's *Theology of Culture*. Tillich writes,

> In order to fulfill his destiny, man must be in possession of creative powers, analogous to those previously attributed to God, and so creativity becomes a human quality....[S]ome may have the strength to take anxiety and meaninglessness courageously

upon themselves and live creatively, expressing the predicament of the most sensitive people in our time in cultural production.... The great works of the visual arts, of music, of poetry, of literature, of architecture, of dance, of philosophy, show in their style both the encounter with non-being, and the strength which can stand this encounter and shape it creatively. Without this key, contemporary culture is a closed door. With this key, it can be understood as the revelation of man's predicament, both in the present world and in the world universally. This makes the protesting element in contemporary culture theologically significant.[1]

"This is powerful," says Banfield. "Let's really think about this: '[S]ome may have the strength to take anxiety and meaninglessness courageously upon themselves and live creatively, expressing the predicament of the most sensitive people in our time in cultural production.'

"Artists help make meaning out of anxiety and meaninglessness. They have the strength to help all of us make meaning out of life, to express 'the predicament of the most sensitive people in our time.' This is so important. 'Without this key, contemporary culture is a closed door.' Without this art, the world today makes no sense. 'With this key,' the world can be understood—it is understood as 'the revelation of man's predicament'—our predicament today and universally."

Banfield argues that artists need courage to call out the ills of society and to challenge wrongs or limitations found in the commercialization of art. Artists need the courage not to "sell out" or create the art that is most easily saleable but has no other social value. They need to create the art that helps the world make sense.

Banfield continues, "If I'm a rapper, that's good news for me, if I'm rapping about drug addiction and abuse and other ills and if I am making sure not to cave to the biases of the industry. Rap that is misogynistic is not courageous.

"If I'm a songwriter, that's good news for me. If I have the courage to deal with issues of justice, that is great. That is courage. These are all the things that it takes courage to do, and that is a critical thing for artists, not just being part of a machine but actually having the courage to call out.

"It takes courage to express art," says Banfield. "Artists are brave people. They are society's heroes."

Time: A Process of Becoming

It takes a long time, a lifetime, to become an artist, says Banfield. In fact, for him, artists are always in the process of "becoming."

Bob Dylan (1941-), born Robert Allen Zimmerman, is a singer-songwriter and one of the most influential figures in American music. His early songs include "Like a Rolling Stone," "The Times They Are A-Changin," and Blowin' in the Wind."

"The artist is involved in discovery, re-discovery, and more discovery, un-discovery, and discovery again. If you look at the progress of any artist's work—Bob Dylan, Prince, Jimi Hendrix, Madonna—and pull that back to Picasso, Richard Wagner, Gertrude Stein, it's the same process.

Prince (1958-), born Prince Rogers Nelson, is a singer and musician who combines R&B, soul, funk, rap, blues, electronica, and jazz.

Jimi Hendrix (1942-1970), born Johnny Allen Hendrix, is considered by some to be the greatest electric guitarist of all time.

Pablo Picasso (1881-1973), a Spanish painter, sculptor, and founder of Cubism, was one of the greatest artists of the 20th century.

Gertrude Stein (1874-1946), was an American writer who spent most of her life in Paris, where she befriended many artists and writers.

"If the artist has a chance to hit the ground, he or she hits the ground with an experiential base, triumphs and challenges, identity crunches, no matter what. Whether the artist is born with a silver spoon in his mouth or eating out of a rusty can, the idea is that those experiences are in his or her human narrative. The artist deals with those experiences, he or she dispels some, comes to grips with some, and the creations are the result of that.

"Now, if people live long enough, they are going to have more triumphs and more struggles, and their art becomes a companion of that narrative. If the person is developing along the historical trajectory of social chaos and social triumph, then that art is going to be reflective and informed by that. That is a point of journey and discovery."

Banfield expresses a concern about television shows like *American Idol*. They give the impression that anyone can become a star in an instant, that artistry is spontaneous and quick, or that it is something imposed upon the artist from the outside—a stamp of approval given by society— by attaining the most call-in votes. As Banfield says, "There is this idea that you can push a button and be an artist. But artistry comes from inner reflection." Still, says Banfield, even though "art is about the inner experience, it must be nurtured." And it grows in relationship to the external world.

Arts education, says Banfield, ought to equip people "to think about their sense and place of themselves as artists, participating in and contributing to culture. Artists need to think critically about the meaning of their art, from the standpoint of an individual and a critical and creative thinker."

Cultural Studies

Banfield teaches what he calls a "cultural studies" approach to art. This approach asks young artists to focus not only on craft or technique, but on themselves, their identity, and their society. This approach benefits all artists, regardless of their discipline, since it takes more than artistic technique to forge a career and to enter the world of artists. It takes an understanding of art's meaning, its function, its purpose, and its goals.

Banfield believes that the young artists he teaches need "a humanities curriculum that engages and refines their thinking as well as the development of their 'inner-core-soul.' Contributing to society as citizens or being socially and politically aware won't seem so distant from their artist-life experience."

Banfield teaches Africana Studies courses that explore the relationships among art, the artist, and society. These courses—The Sociology of Black Music in American Culture, The Theology of American Popular Music, Biographies in Black (Music, Lives, and Meanings)—ask students to think, discuss, and debate the implications, effects, and meanings of cultural expression and phenomena.

Students explore the development of African-American and popular music, in terms of what they reveal about American society—socially, spiritually, politically, and culturally. An important aspect of this exploration is the consideration of the aesthetic and cultural dimensions of African-American life and culture, western conceptions of art, and the social and political contexts that shape music. An important part of the classroom experience is critical discussion. Students are expected to discuss at length and in depth selected musical works, transcriptions, and lyrics.

Students also explore music through the cultural studies lenses of race, ethnicity, gender, sexuality, power, and class. In this way, students listen to, as well as read, write, and think about the way that music interacts with other arts, with people, and with the larger world. Students also explore music through a study of identity—the identity of the musicians and also their own identities.

Self: Who Am I As an Artist

Helping people understand the ways that their personal identities relate to, inform, and infuse their art is one of Banfield's goals. "Artistic identity is important. Who am I as a creator?"

Banfield explains that identity is not fixed and absolute, but is a process for everyone, especially for artists. "Artistry is an evolution. I don't think any of us start with a clear picture of that. Someone or something inspires you. You grow as an artist. It is like a plant. It breathes. It grows. If you are young and you are nurtured in your artistry, you come out better. If one is open, he or she will grow."

Banfield grew up in Detroit. He reminisces: "I grew up in an urban area that was constructed to be wide. In Detroit in those days, in the 1960s and 70s, a young person could grow up to be wide—could attach himself to all different kinds of artists.

"Artists sometimes talk about arts as if we live in an elitist world. But in Detroit, I learned about art in school, in public education. We had great art and music teachers. We were drawing and painting and we had literature and so on. We had a great public education.

"In addition, I had a home, a mother and a father who were very open. They nurtured my brothers and me and they brought all kinds of things to the table—art, music, and a focus on church and school. And they took us to cultural activities that really made a difference for us.

"A turning point for me came when I saw Jimi Hendrix. I saw this guy who looked like me, playing this instrument in a fascinating innovative way, and I said, 'Wow! I want to do that. And that was the guitar, rock and roll.'

"From Jimi Hendrix, I went to jazz, and that inspired me to want to be a creative person. And then I started to appreciate broader arts—museums, poetry, and more.

Community and Computers

"Now this is part of my philosophy. I always believed that there was a connection between what the arts allow us to see in the world and in our ourselves. All artists are concerned about being able to express their own voices, about the relationship between their inner world and the outer world."

Banfield compares the experience of learning about music today, in a world mediated by the computer, with his own experiences, in the "Album Age."

Then, says Banfield, "You had to look at the record and the album cover. You were looking at the paper, at what had been written. It was this big thing. You could hold it in your hand, and you could sit down and listen to it for three hours, for five hours."

As Banfield remembers it, community was almost built into the experience of listening to an album. The record player, the only one in the home, was in a common area—a living room or a parlor. The whole family and sometimes the whole neighborhood would listen to the music together. Listeners would read the album cover and notes, discuss the music and the artists.

Listening to the music was an event that involved sharing and built community. Perhaps unconsciously it also led to an understanding of who one was and one's place in the world. Banfield remembers listening to Stevie Wonder's *Songs in the Key of Life* over and over and over. "We sat there—my friends and me—and it took almost the whole day. This was who we *were*.

"But this is not how young people listen to music today" says Banfield. With the Internet, with what Banfield

refers to as "this box" — the computer — students experience music as individuals. The communal feeling that grew from listening to a whole album with a group of friends is no longer there. Today, the concept of the album — or even the CD — is nearly gone. People listen to a song at a time. They download it, listen with earphones through their computer or MP3 player. "The box gives people a one-stop place for culture," says Banfield. "Everything is in this box."

According to Banfield, the community that comes through "the box" is different than the community built through the shared experience of those friends in the living room. People today have much more choice about who to communicate with, if anyone. Sharing can be done with friends and contacts from around the globe. It can be personal or impersonal. The communications are brief. Asks Banfield, "How do we harness this great energy, this great innovation? How do educators and older artists help young artists today come to understand themselves and their community as it is mediated, fragmented, and framed by this box?"

Banfield continues, "Young people know a lot about what they are seeing in the world. Older artists have to give the younger ones the tools that we have, and we also have to respect young artists. We have to allow them to go out and shape the new world. The old paradigms have shifted and not kinda, sort of, but they have radically changed across the board. And I think we, as educators, are constantly being challenged by that, and we have to take a positive read on this to see that it is great."

One of the key ways that Banfield believes educators can help young artists is by providing — and sometimes requiring — space for reflection, space to slow down, space to stop the fragmentation and explore what one's values are: How does an artist starting out today want to impact his or her world? What are the values that shape that impact?

Document the Culture: Understanding Your Values

Banfield shares a lesson he learned from his mentor Dr. Thomas Jefferson "T.J." Anderson, a composer, conductor, orchestrator, and educator well-known for his orchestration of the Scott Joplin opera, *Tremonisha*. Banfield was privileged to study with Anderson, who served as a Professor of Music at Tufts University, until he retired in 1990.

"T.J. taught me that the duty of the artist is to document the culture," says Banfield. "So your music or your painting, your dance, your poetry is supposed to document the world that is going on."

But, today, for Banfield, docu- mentation alone is not enough. "A lot of rappers would say I am just documenting my world, so if there is violence in my music, it is because there is violence in the world. But artists need to learn what to do with their documentation." The artist cannot simply accept violence or the way record corporations exploit that violence in the interest of sales. An artist needs to make a mark on the world that relates to his or her values and asks people to think about their world in new ways.

Banfield elaborates with another lesson he learned from Dr. Anderson, about creativity and the artist's role in society: "T.J. would say, 'Everybody in the bathtub is creative. The man singing in the bathtub is creative. The difference between that creative man singing in the bathtub and you is that you know what to do with that creativity. You understand that your art has a purpose.'"

An artist knows that art is not about personal vanity—it is not about what will make the artist famous. It is about making a mark on the world, expressing the unexpressed. To reference Tillich again, art provides the key to contemporary culture's "closed door."

Continues Banfield, "T.J. taught me the difference between the person who is just interested in winning and the artist who knows what his purpose is. An artist knows what to do with his or her creativity. An artist knows how to use his or her gift."

For Banfield, coming to understand the function of his "gift" led him to see that technical and music study was not enough. To understand better his place in the world, his relationship with others, and the role of his art, he decided to study theology and philosophy.

Worldview: Africa, Wagner, Race and the Academy

A trip to Africa during his master's program in theology was, for Banfield, life-changing and, as he explains, "allowed me to develop a global understanding of music, spirituality, and communal art. I came to see an important part of how the larger world, the majority culture, does music and culture and life."

Banfield, working on his masters at the time, was part of a mission trip to Dakar, Senegal, traveling with a team of musicians and doctors. "I had the intention of using Africa as a model for what I called 'theological music.' I went with the idea of exploring the relationship among theology, music, and social justice. We taught American music to African musicians, and they taught us their music. We would practice in the day, give concerts at night, and have a kind of cultural exchange. The doctors took medical supplies and gave care.

"I had never been to Africa. I didn't know what to expect. We got into these trucks and went way into the interior of the country. This was modern Africa in the late 1980s. The people—women and children mostly—immediately came out to the cars, forming a circle around us. Not told we were going to be there, not knowing we were musicians, they would sing their songs for us. They weren't told to have a ceremony. This is just what they did. This is the culture. Then the women would get the leaders of the community to come and meet our group. That was my experience. In the evenings, we would work with this great choir director. We would teach them. They would teach us.

"There were a lot of other wonderful pieces to that. Older Africans would say, 'Don't ever forget you are African. You are at home here. You represent us in that wild place called America.' An old woman told me that I looked just like her nephew. In America, the melting pot, they tell you to erase that.

"America is about ethnic washing away in place of this American identity which is supposedly one homogeneous people. That is a beautiful thing in one way, but if you are African-American, these identities have to get a shaking, sometimes beautiful and comfortable and sometimes not.

"When you are in that situation of the cultural identity crush, of what it means to be American, and you go to the ethnic origins of your identity, in this case, to Africa, it is a humbling and beautiful experience. For me, it was revelatory and ushered in a whole new sense of self.

"I am African-American, but I only knew the American part. I didn't know the African part. In a way my feelings were like a cliché, but they were real. You see these films, when African-Americans arrive in Africa for the first time, and they say, 'Oh, my God, I'm home,' and it seems like TV melodrama, but that is exactly how I experienced it. I really felt, 'Oh, my God, I'm home,' and the Africans I met said to me, 'Oh, yes, you're home.' You would see people, and everyone looks like you.

"That experience allowed me to shape, in a whole different way, my approach to art. I realized that art is completely bound up with identity and culture. But my thesis advisor at Boston University hated the theory and refused to pass me, saying that what I was arguing could not be proven. My advisor would not accept the theories that I learned in Africa, theories which are now the foundation of cultural studies. Those very things I argued, questions of identity shaping art, they said that those things would never fly in the academy.

"I took another year and reformulated my work. I was required to base my thesis on Western Europe. In the end, I wrote a better thesis: I argued that it is a universal truth that art is shaped by culture and impacts society, but since you will not let me say this about Africa, I will say it about Western European music.

"I chose to study Richard Wagner, who believed that he was going to humanize the world through opera. He had the King of Bavaria build him a huge theater, which he could use to highlight German culture. He had no intention of it being used for Nazism, although he had his own problems with the racial and cultural tracts that he wrote. Wagner was a scoundrel of a human being but his music was absolutely beautiful.

"My theory of aesthetics grew out of this exploration—looking at Wagner's relationship to culture, as well as the relationship of African culture to African music, my relationship to popular music based on my experience as a Motown person, seeing how that music grew from that community. This began my exploration into cultural studies."

Art and Being

To revise his thesis, Banfield took a one-year deferment to hold his place in the doctoral program at the University of Michigan. "It was painful," he remembers, "but I answered important questions and I figured out what my battlegrounds with the academy were going to be.

"That is why I tell students that, from their struggles, they will grow. Everyone has to learn how to turn those lemons into lemonade. That year allowed me to have a clear idea of what I wanted to focus on in the doctoral program and in my work since then: How does an artifact speak? What does it tell you about the art maker? The framer? All of these values are embedded in a piece of art. When you see a piece of art, when you listen to a composition, you see the frame of reference about how art is constructed. This is the basis of artistic creation. It is the connection, the expression of the artist's identity and culture.

"Artists need to know who they are if they are going to be able to create art that matters.

"Art enables us to understand ourselves and our world," says Banfield. "Art enables us to see who we are, why we are, and what we mean to each other."

"Art tells us about the power of being. Through it, we express our humanity."

Note

[1] Tillich, Paul. *Theology of Culture*. NY Oxford UP, 1959. pp. 44, 46-47. Print.

CHAPTER 4

Michael Bearden

Photo used with permission.

Being True to Yourself

Musical director, keyboardist, and composer Michael Bearden is the band leader for the TBS late night show Lopez Tonight. *He served as Musical Director for the "This Is It" concert series Michael Jackson had planned to hold in London before his untimely death in 2009. Bearden is featured in the documentary film* This Is It, *for which he also served as music supervisor, composer, and associate film producer.*

Bearden has worked with Christina Aguilera, Ricky Martin, Destiny's Child, D'Angelo, Marc Dorsey, Faith Evans, Brian McKnight, Mary J. Blige, Herbie Hancock, Rod Stewart, and Jennifer Lopez. He has performed and/or recorded with Madonna, Whitney Houston, Lionel Richie, Chaka Khan, Patti Austin, James Ingram, Babyface, Lenny Kravitz, Yoko Ono, George Benson, Natalie Cole, Sophie B. Hawkins, Anita Baker, Edie Brickell, Nancy Wilson, Stevie Wonder, Aretha Franklin, Liza Minnelli, and Ray Charles.

Bearden has scored the films Drop Squad, The Visit, Arrangement, One Week, *and* Redrum. *He has also scored several documentaries, ABC's* Swingtown, *CW's* The Game, *and HBO's* Brave New Voices. *He was the principal pianist/keyboardist in two* Bill Cosby *television show bands and has performed frequently with the band on CBS's* Late Show with David Letterman. *Bearden was also principal keyboardist for President Barack Obama's 2009 inaugural concert at the Lincoln Memorial.*

Bearden earned a bachelor's degree from Howard University and serves on the Board of Governors of The Recording Academy-the Los Angeles Chapter.

In this chapter, Bearden discusses the importance of being oneself in one's art.

Michael Bearden's life sounds a bit like a rags-to-riches story, a common plot line in literature, where a neighborhood child rises from simple circumstances to fame. But for Bearden, the tale is true.

With his boyish grin, Bearden looks out from under his cap, and in a soft-spoken voice, begins: "I was raised on the south side of Chicago. That is where I grew up." The south side has a reputation for being poor, but Bearden didn't feel at all deprived as a child. His father is a teacher in the Chicago area, and is also an artist. "We did not have a lot of money," says Bearden, "but we had a lot of love in the house, and I had support for my music. This was very important to me.

"I have known that I wanted to play music since I was two years old," he explains, and he has stayed committed to this goal. "I had a baby-sitter who played Aretha Franklin records all the time and that got me hooked. At five, I began playing the piano. Keyboards are like my little Linus blanket, my safety net, the way I interact with the world. I was lucky. I knew early on what I wanted to do with the rest of my life and I had parents who supported me."

Aretha Franklin (1942-), an American singer and songwriter often referred to as the Queen of Soul, has had 20 number one R&B singles.

Bearden shows the positive results that come from support and focus, as well as commitment to a dream. He has taken to heart every lesson and idea he has learned about music, from the age of two to the present, for he believes that he is always learning. Since childhood, Bearden has understood that music is as much about performance skills as it is about understanding people and about discipline. He has concentrated on finding his own voice and not letting others sidetrack him, or lessen his commitment to his goals.

"Where I grew up in Chicago, the piano was not considered a mas-culine instrument—it wasn't macho. We had gangs and all the turmoil of the inner city. We had distractions, but, with my parents' help, I stayed clear of them."

Bearden was an excellent student and received a scholarship to Howard University in Washington, D.C. There, he says, he met "a lot of talented peo-ple, artists, and friends. I was able to hone my craft and train."

After graduating from college, Bearden moved to Brooklyn, to what he describes as "a three-story walk-up, with a bathroom down the hall that I shared with two families." He laughs, "I wanted to make my way in New York and that is what I did.

Herbie Mann (1930-2003), born Herbert Jay Solomon, was a Jewish-American flutist and one of the first musicians to fuse jazz and world music.

Stanley Turrentine (1934-2000) was an American tenor saxophonist, known for his contributions to soul jazz and jazz fusion.

Freddie Hubbard (1938-2008) was an American jazz trumpeter, known primarily for playing in the bebop and post-bop styles from the 1960s.

Angela Bofill (1954-), an American singer and songwriter, was one of the first Latina vocalists to achieve success in the R&B market.

"I got a job with the great flut-ist Herbie Mann. That was my first break. Through him, I met Stanley Turrentine and Freddie Hubbard. I started playing with all those people.

"It did not pay much, not re-ally what I needed to survive in New York," he continues, "so I did other small jobs. I started work-ing with singers like Angela Bofill. This opened up a whole new audi-ence, a whole new revenue stream, and new genres.

"From there, I was invited to audition to play with Whitney Houston. And I got the gig. Once I was with Whitney, everything just took off. We did the Super Bowl. Whitney introduced me to a lot of people. From her, I went straight to Madonna."

Whitney Houston (1963-), often referred to as a "singer's singer," reached number one on *Billboard's* Hot 100 a record seven consecutive times.

Bearden describes his introduction to Madonna: "She wanted to meet musicians to play with her one time on *Saturday Night Live.* There was no audition involved. She wanted to look at us. She chose me. I don't really know why. We did that one show together, and she was impressed. She asked me, 'What are you doing for the summer?' and I told her, 'I am going on tour with you.' She laughed, but that was the beginning of a long professional relationship. After that tour, she asked me to be her musical director. I accepted, and we spent nine years together.

"Then I met Michael Jackson and I did the 30th anniversary tour with him in 2001. I played with every artist in the show, especially Michael and his brothers.

Michael Jackson (1958-2009) was a singer, songwriter, and dancer, whose album *Thriller* is the best-selling album of all time.

"At that same time, I was just starting to work with Jennifer Lopez. I did a lot of other albums and was quite busy. I started back with Michael Jackson for the *This Is It* tour. And we all know what happened there. Now I am musical director for George Lopez, a talk show on TBS, called *Lopez Tonight.*

Jennifer Lopez (1969-) is an American singer and actress who has earned a total of nine top ten hits, including four number one singles.

George Lopez (1961-) is a Mexican-American comedian who starred in his own sitcom and hosted a late-night talk show, *Lopez Tonight.*

Lionel Richie (1949-), an American singer and songwriter, originally with the Commodores, has written more than twenty top-10 hits.

Understanding People

Despite his many accomplishments and the time he has spent working with world-class artists, Bearden is humble. "A lot of people ask me why I am so low-key. I think it is the way that I was raised. I learned early on that I wanted to be proud of myself and of my music. Even now, I stay focused on what is important and try not to get caught up in the glitz.

"I am also a calm person, and that is how I handle my business. A dear musician friend of mine told me that it is better to maintain the relationship with the person than to be right. Even if the point is right, it is better to be humble about it and to maintain the personal connection. I have taken this to heart.

"It is absolutely imperative that you have good people skills, if you want to be a working musician or a musical director, or any kind of working artist," he explains. "Lionel Richie and I were talking about these very things once. We were putting together a project. He mentioned that he was working with someone who is very, very talented. Lionel could get what he wanted from that person. But he did not like him. He was not a good person for Lionel to work with.

Liza Minnelli (1946-), the daughter of Judy Garland and director Vincente Minnelli, is an American actor and singer, who won an Oscar for *Cabaret*.

"Nobody cares how well you can play if you're not good to work with. If you're a jerk and you can't make it on time or you don't dress appropriately, if you don't know when to voice your opinion and when to keep it to yourself, you won't get called back. There will be somebody who can do all those things, who is easy to work with and professional. And so, to be personable, do the gig, and be humble about it is absolutely vital and necessary to work.

"Some people said that I would not survive Madonna or Michael Jackson, or Liza Minnelli, or some other artists who have reputations for being demanding. But I had no problem with anyone. In fact, I found Madonna to be quite refreshing as an artist, because of her hands-on work ethic. She works as hard as anyone I have ever met, if not harder. I love that because there is no guess work.

Bearden adds, "I don't have a sense of entitlement. I see my working with these stars as a privilege and I try to live up to that. It is how I was raised to be."

Mentors

In addition to his parents, Bearden credits several teachers and mentors with his success. "The thing about any apprenticeship is that you do not realize what you are being prepared for when you are in it, especially if you are a child," he explains. "But I can absolutely credit three main pillars or catalysts, people who really catapulted me into becoming the person that I am now.

"The first is my elementary school band director, Mr. William Leslie. I was playing piano at five years old, so by the time I got to first grade, I knew a lot about music. But there was a young lady in my elementary school, a girl a little older than I was. By the time I got there, she had the piano part.

"I had to choose another instrument, but I didn't know what to choose. Mr. Leslie said, 'You look like you could be a drummer.' I took his word for it and started playing drums. From there, I learned a lot about rhythm and feeling and how to anchor a band. This is essential to what I do now, when I lead a band.

"Mr. Leslie was a wonderful leader and supporter, one of my biggest cheerleaders. Throughout my elementary school career, he was there. He came with me when I had to audition for my high school."

Bearden attended Whitney M. Young High School, Chicago's first magnet high school. There, he met First Lady Michelle Obama. They are still friends to this day. "It is quite surreal to have someone you know so intimately be the First Lady of the United States," says Bearden.

His high school band director, Ivory Brock, was also key to Bearden's development. "Because of him," says Bearden, "I developed as a band leader and as a leader, period. He taught me how to take music and my ambitions more seriously. He was a big influence. I was a section leader in the band, in concert band, and on the drum line. He taught me marimba, timpani, and other percussion instruments.

"He would never let me just be content. When I thought I was good, he would throw something else on me. He would never let me rest."

At Howard, "my major was music education," explains Bearden. "My parents always wanted me to have a fall back—so I majored in education. But I hate the term 'fall back,'" Bearden continues. "Fall to me means fail—and I had no intention of failing. I never really wanted to become a teacher. I was a piano major as well, so I was able to play, and that was what I wanted to do."

Fred Irby, III—Director of the Howard University Jazz Ensemble, Professor of Music, Coordinator of Instrumental Music, Trumpet Instructor, and Principal Trumpet player of the Kennedy Center Opera House Musical Theater Orchestra—was a powerful influence on Bearden at Howard. Bearden explains, "Mr. Irby is an A-list trumpet player and gets called for every show in D.C. I have worked several jobs with him since I graduated. He always introduces me and he always tells everyone in the orchestra, 'This is my student.' He is so proud. We do the Christmas in Washington show together every year at the National Museum. We do a lot of shows together.

"These three men were my main teachers and influences. I look back on them and thank them, even to this day," says Bearden. "They set me on my path."

Clear Path and Passion

Bearden never doubted his path. "If you want to be a musician, an artist," he adds, "you have to dedicate yourself to music, to your art. You've got to have a passion for it. It has be something that you would want to do for free—and I've done it for free," he laughs. "There were absolutely low points, extreme low points, where I was not hired for a job and the money that I was making was not enough to sustain. In those moments, you can't go away from what you do. In those moments, those times of greatest challenge, you have to figure out a different way to reach your goals.

"This is true for all musicians. You can't just play. You have to be able to do whatever you can do in music—play, arrange, compose, engineer, sound design, whatever it is. For me, when one thing was not working, in those very low moments, I just concentrated on another aspect of my craft.

"Those low moments came, but I never wanted to give up my art. I never even thought about it. Although I am successful now, I was not at the beginning. I just tried to make provisions while I was working to prepare for the times when I may not be. I still do this."

Connecting the Arts

Bearden also notes how important it is for artists to develop beyond their primary art. Musicians need to develop all their musicianship skills, and they need to explore other art genres as well. All artists need to develop an appreciation for and understanding of a range of art forms. "This will help your career," Bearden says.

"Musicians can have a tendency to concentrate only on music and to care really only about that. They sometimes don't see the relationship between music and other arts, such as dance, drama, and stage production. Knowledge of all of these arts helps you as you develop your own personal art. Look at Michael Jackson," Bearden says. "He could do it all. He was a dancer and actor as much as he was a musician. He was an amazing dancer.

"As a musician, you need to appreciate other performing arts especially. For example, if you are working with an actor who can project only past a certain number of people, knowing that will help you in your musical performance. You will create your music so that you do not drown out the actor. Likewise, if you know that certain dramatic events are going to happen on stage, it will help you shape your music. If you know that certain tempos are too fast for certain dance moves, it will help you shape your playing. There are a lot of subtle things that you need to learn to know how the pieces fit together.

"You don't have to study in-depth the arts beyond your primary one. A musician doesn't have to be the lighting director, for instance, but you should know what is involved.

"When I score films," Bearden continues, "I find that there are not a lot of directors who know much about music. They know a lot about films, but don't have a clue about music. To me, that is wrong. When they are writing, they should know what a scene might look like, what it might sound like, and how it might feel with certain music.

"The filmmakers I know who understand music—like Spike Lee or Martin Scorsese—who absolutely know about music, you can see why their films are so great."

Greatest Accomplishments

Bearden has seen great success but believes that he has not yet achieved his "greatest accomplishment." He explains,

Herbie Hancock (1940-) is an American pianist and composer, who infuses jazz with funk, soul, rock, blues, and classical music.

"I still have not reached where I want to be. I have had some great milestones. Herbie Hancock is a great mentor and he heavily influenced me. I had his posters on my wall when I was a kid." A great moment came when Bearden worked with Hancock on the 2005 album *Possibilities*. "It blows my mind that right now I can text him and he would hit me back. He is a personal hero and it was a milestone to work with him," says Bearden.

"Working with Michael Jackson on his final triumph, that was a milestone, too," Bearden continues. "Not what I thought, of course, when I began working with him on the *This Is It* tour.

"It is tragic, the loss of M.J., the loss of my friend, and the loss of this musical genius. But through the film *This Is It*, we touched more people than we were probably going to through the shows. In a weird way, out of tragedy came some light and love and healing that we did not expect. One of my biggest accomplishments is probably working on this film, sharing Michael's legacy. It has touched so many people all around the world, that it is overwhelming. I get notes and emails from my fan base. It is quite amazing."

Another milestone for Bearden was the 2009 Presidential Inauguration Concert. "I played for Barack and Michelle Obama," says Bearden. "It was quite surreal to have your friends be the most powerful couple in the world.

"Before I performed, I was in my hotel room with a doctor and had an IV coming out of my arm. I had a 102 degree fever. I was so sick. It was crazy. But I would not let that stop me. I was there.

"The President and First Lady were so shocked. They did not know that I was going to be there. They were excited. It was wonderful to be on the steps where Martin Luther King gave his 'I Have a Dream' speech, to look at all those millions of people. I felt a way that I cannot really express. I am a Black man. To have a Black man be the president of the United States, the first one, that is something monumental, that was great."

Bearden adds, "I just try to do good work. What has been most rewarding for me is how people have reacted to the work that I have done already."

Identity

Bearden does not consciously try to communicate, as he puts it, "any kind of social message through my art. I just do it. The thing I have found," he adds, "is if you try to go for a certain thing, it won't happen. If I try to put forward some big message, I don't think it would work.

"The thing I have learned from my dad is that talk is cheap. It is what you *do* that counts. So if you are talking a good game but you are not doing what you are saying, it doesn't even matter. I pretty much let the art speak for itself.

"The fact that I am a Black man comes through. I am an example. George Lopez and I talk about this kind of thing a lot. He calls himself Chicano, and he says, 'Man, we are on this show together [TBS' *Lopez Tonight*] and we are doing well in the ratings.' George has a keen eye on history and what it means. He says, 'Man, we are in the history annals with Johnny Carson and Jack Parr. I am the first Mexican-American to have my face on late night and I have a Black musical director.' That is pretty deep."

"Even if we don't think about it, or say anything about it, the person who is ten years old or fifteen or even eighteen to thirty-four who is watching, will be inspired, not necessarily to be a musician, but to do whatever—maybe to be the president or the first woman president or whatever it is. In a way, we are role models. I don't take that lightly.

Jack Paar (1918-2004) was an American radio and television comedian best known for hosting *The Tonight Show* from 1957 to 1962.

Johnny Carson (1925-2005) was an American comedian who hosted *The Tonight Show Starring Johnny Carson* for thirty years, from 1962-92.

"Everything that I do, I realize could be influencing somebody. I try to make it be the best that it can be. That is the only statement that I try to make. The fact that I am Black should not matter, although it still does."

Be True to Yourself

"The main thing that helps me," he adds, "is to be sincere and true to yourself, whatever that is. Study other people, but don't sound like them or try to be them. Be yourself. You can study Herbie Hancock, like I did, but I don't sound like him. You have to take what you have learned and be true to yourself. Learn from others *and* make your own voice. It is easier to be yourself than try to put on a mask and be someone else. You can't keep that up.

"Nobody can be you better than you can. So be yourself. Find out what that is and be that. And the good thing

Janis Joplin (1943-1970) was an American singer and songwriter, whose biggest hit, "Me and Bobby McGee," came after her death at age 27.

about art is that whatever that is, you will be right. Some people love Bob Dylan's voice and some people hate it. Some people love his writing and some people hate it. Some people love Janis Joplin's voice. Some people love Whitney Houston's voice, but some people don't. The thing is they are all right.

"Everyone has to be able to make their way and win their own audience. Be you. Don't try to be anyone else. Be yourself."

CHAPTER 5

Caroline Harvey

Photo used with permission.

Claiming Your Art and Transforming Lives

Caroline Harvey is a poet and performer who has appeared on HBO's Def Poetry Jam and has competed nationally on the poetry slam circuit. She is also a dancer and yoga expert; a yoga, dance, and meditation instructor and workshop leader; and a doula (birth attendant). She is in private practice as a Somatic Therapist, specializing in Craniosacral Therapy, and is the creator of Sacred Groove™, an ecstatic dance practice, Awakening the Yogini: Extraordinary Yoga and Education for Women™, and The CranioYoga Work: The Artful Synthesis of Restorative Yin Yoga and CranioSacral Therapy™.

Harvey earned a Bachelor of Fine Arts in Theater from Boston University, a Master's Degree in Dance from the University of California Los Angeles's Department of World Arts and Cultures, and is also a graduate of the Massage Therapy Institute of Davis, California. A devoted student of health and yoga pioneer Ana Forrest, Harvey serves as a teaching assistant for the Upledger Institute for Craniosacral Therapy. A registered member of the United States Association for Body Psychotherapists, Harvey has studied closely with bodywork and movement innovator Julian Walker, the Women's Sacred Anatomy Project founder Ellen Heed, the Center for Movement Education and Research founder and director Judy Gantz, and the Men's Yoga Tribe founder Jonathan Bowra.

In this chapter, Harvey explains how, through her art, she is able to explore her authentic self. Finding her voice and helping others find theirs is key to her work.

Caroline Harvey's path to artistry has been as non-traditional as her current artistic practice. She sees herself as a person who "has always had to make my own way." She is a writer, dancer, spoken word performer, yoga instructor, somatic therapist, and more. She has what she calls a "portfolio career," making her living and practicing her art in her own unique and diverse way.

For Harvey, what is most important about her art is expressing her authentic self and helping others "heal" by exploring theirs. She sees art and art making as transformative processes, ones that help people understand themselves and lead healthier, more holistic lives. As a performer on stage, and working one-on-one with individuals, her goal is to help people grow internally, find themselves, and feel whole.

> Somatic therapy—therapy of or related to the body as well as to the mind—is a holistic therapy that integrates the mental, emotion, spiritual, and physical.

She recalls a shift in her work as she matured as an artist, when her "artistry started to support and blend with the healing arts." Her practice continued to include performance, but also began to include what she describes as "interpersonal and personal work and transformation," where she is "not just doing this thing before an audience but also working with people individually."

Harvey credits two people with influencing her path. First is her grandfather—the famed civil and human rights attorney Arthur Harvey, who represented artists like Paul Robeson at a time when doing so made him a target for the McCarthy hearings. "I jokingly say this but it is also kind of true," Harvey explains, "that everything I learned about performance, I learned from watching the trial attorneys in my family. There are no higher stakes than summations at a criminal trial."

Paul Robeson (1898-1976) was an African-American actor, singer, and political activist. The first Black actor to portray Shakespeare's Othello on Broadway, he fell victim to the anti-communist scare in the 1950s and faced unfair accusation from U.S. Senator Joseph McCarthy.

She continues, "My grandfather was Jewish from Brooklyn. His father came over from Russia. He had this outspoken personality and a really sharp mind. He did tons of work with artists, people of color, and Jews in the early 1950s. For him, it was really about right versus wrong. It was just a moral compass that he lived by. He would distinguish the bull from what was right and choose the right way to go.

"My grandfather set a really beautiful tone that got carried to my father. My mother also has that vibe. Her side of the family, back a generation or two, had a traveling circus. So growing up with these outspoken legacies being really celebrated, with these as the stories around the dinner table—like when Grandpa said, 'F--- you to the McCarthy hearing,'—those stories were formative."

When she was a teen, Harvey took to heart all that she had learned from her family about subversion. As she recalls, "I drove my parents totally insane, challenging them all the time. They would jokingly say, 'Why did we tell her all those stories?'"

Determined to make her own way in the world, Harvey left high school at fifteen to follow The Grateful Dead around the country. She eventually relocated to England to study creative writing, art history, and philosophy at Oxford Tutorial College. After studying and traveling in Europe and North America, she lived for a time in Colorado and then moved to Boston. She studied theater and dance at Boston University, where she earned her bachelor's degree. From there, she went to the University of California Los Angeles, to earn a master's degree in dance.

The second person Harvey credits with helping to form her artistic practice is theater revolutionary Peter Sellars, professor of World Arts and Cultures at UCLA, where he teaches *Art as Social Action* and *Art as*

Moral Action.

"I was in Sellars' graduate course called 'Gestures of Compassion,'" Harvey explains. "At that time, the department was in transition. It was a fledgling dance program that was on its way to becoming a World Dance and Culture Department. It had been mostly focused on dance therapy, and then it became a program reflective of performance and dance as a whole.

> The Grateful Dead, an American rock band formed in 1965, was known for its unique and eclectic style, which fused rock, folk, bluegrass, blues, reggae, and country.

> Peter Sellars (1957-) is an American theater director known for his unconventional stagings of Shakespeare and other classical theatrical works. in 1998 and the Dorothy and Lillian Gish Prize in 2005.

The semester before I had to write my thesis, I signed up for Sellars' class. The focus was on compassion—what is a gesture of compassion. We explored compassion through all five senses."

For Harvey, the course was "this totally mind blowing experience of gathering creative people around a concept and exploring it in detail: How we could exist in the world together; What is our function as artists?; What is compassionate service?; How do we serve?

"It shifted everything for me. It was one of those classes where you leave in tears and you think, 'Oh, did that just happen?' You can't believe it."

From Images to Words

For Harvey, words and movement are the media she uses most often to express what is important to her and her art. But her thinking—her artistic practice—usually begins with a concept or an image.

She explains, "The place I end up landing is writing and word-related arts. But while creating for me involves words, it usually begins with a visual image that I can see in my mind. That envisioning is a big part of my process. I work with images, and I write from images. And for me the writing is really connected with movement and live physical expression and movement. In my process, in my brain, everything feels really interrelated."

In fact, her most recent series of poems focuses on the women in the paintings of Salvador Dali. They come to life and speak—are transformed from image through Harvey's words Harvey shares one below.

The Desire of Dali's Women

for the women he painted

You will imagine me
reckless, lightning-eyed,
smelling like
burn.

You will imagine me
falling, windswept, gone and
gone and
gone and O,
O, how you will fester at the ambiguity of my
mouth.

One day you will decide
it suits you best to kiss a woman
whose face is not the moon
but rather the earth,
so you will dust my cheeks with orchid blooms,
sculpt me a grasp of roses instead of teeth.
You will wrap my roots around
your neck, my thorns will stick to your
mustache, I will grow a tiny vegetable garden on
my tongue.

You will come,
again and again, you will come.
Clutch of pen, clutch of carving knife,
and you will cut hallow
caverns where my breasts and heart should be.
You will slough my skin from bone,
set fire to my legs,
tie me to stone,
loose dogs upon me,
and I will stand
as motionless as cooled bronze,
as still as your grey, lifeless planks of ground.

You fear that I might toss you in your sleep:
that I might be the lucid vision to
shake awake the unhinged you,
the way your mama shook you crazy when
you were young.

You fear that I might
rattle this ripped stretch of canvas
and beg my maker for
something wet and malleable,
but I don't dream of hot, quick things
the way you imagine most women do.
I don't beg for liberation.
Not from god.
Not from you.

I am wild.
And I will demand that you know me.
But not for the swirl that catches you at introduction,
not for the shift of hair you name *mother* or *home* or *muse*.
Those are the tedious things of first drafts,
that's child's play,
so let them have it.

You and I, we are
man and we are woman.
But we are not lifelong.
We are not growing old.
We are not graveside together.
O Dali,
O Precious One,
O heaving, huddled runt of a man!
You already know this woman,
so paint me.
But paint me as I am:
paint me with a mouth.
Paint me with teeth.
Paint me with a face.
Paint me with legs.
Paint me with hands.
Paint me with breath.
Paint me with eyes.
Paint me with feet.
Paint me with legs.
Paint me with a mouth.
Paint me with teeth.
Paint me with breath.
Paint me with blood.
Paint me with a mouth.
Paint me with teeth.

Paint me with a mouth.
Paint me with a mouth.

I won't be still, I won't be silent.
I won't be still, I won't be silent.
I won't be still, I won't be silent for you anymore,
Maestro.

Communication

In her art, says Harvey, "I am really passionate about communicating something that feels vital and important and potentially transformational. In my process, I try not to limit myself. I am going to learn whatever languages I can to communicate and to reveal something important about the human condition."

Salvador Dali (1904-1989), one of the masters of 20th century art, is considered the greatest artist of the surrealist movement. Surrealism—meaning, literally, more than real or beyond real—was an art movement heavily influenced by the theories of Dr. Sigmund Freud. Dali strove to paint the unconscious mind that is recalled during dreams. His 1931 work, *The Persistence of Memory*, featuring melting clocks, is probably his most famous painting.

Harvey thinks of her poetry and of art making as "a ceremony." She speaks often of the role of the master of ceremonies or emcee, a role she takes on when she hosts a spoken word performance or poetry slam. "My writing," she says, "is where I am strongest. It is where my brain clicks in a way that is most clear and effortless and in the end, feels the most fun for me. But I want to be involved in creating moments that help things shift or create a journey where the performer and audience are transformed from one place to another. It is writing but it is really communicating."

For Harvey, words come to life in the performance. "I have felt for a long time that my art was most true around live performance. I am trying to soften around this. I am trying to branch out to publishing and actual page writing."

She explains the hesitation she feels when she takes a poem from the stage to the page. "Formats that document the work always feel to me a little like some of the vital things have been shaved off. It feels like the word on the page is missing the breath of the word in my mouth on stage. And the movement, the energetic exchange, and the eye contact are missing. I look at the words printed in the book and think: 'That looks nice, that is okay,' but it will be a million times more powerful when it has the body with it."

Harvey believes her art is most powerful and her communication is richest during live performance. "Video feels okay, but it also flattens. You miss something. I miss something. I really miss the live breath connection that happens between the performer and the audience.

"The connection—when you are in a room and get really moved by what is happening, and the performer is just as moved as the audience—that delineation fades away in a live performance and everyone is really ecstatic about that transformation."

For Harvey, finding your voice and being transformed are the true purposes of art.

A Stand-up Poet—Writing, Dancing, and More

Harvey remembers, as a child, thinking, "I want to be a stand-up poet. Is that a thing? I didn't know that you could perform as a poet. It was later in life that I discovered that there were other people doing that and obviously ancient civilizations of people doing that."

She began writing at a very young age. "I was already writing poems and plays and musicals when I was five or six years old. So I have always done that."

She also began dancing when she was very young. "Dance, too," she recalls, "has been always with me. Technique and formal dancing training came right around the same time as writing. They were always happening together."

At age six, Harvey began formal study in jazz, ballet, and tap. "I stayed with ballet until age fifteen, then I moved to modern dance and flamenco. I also have been studying yoga since age eight. Every summer I went to a performing arts camp that had really eclectic offerings, including dance and theater, both musical theater and drama.

"My undergraduate program was in the arts, not so much classical dance training but more on theater and movement for actors. I began formal dance training again in graduate school, in a program that focused on world culture and dance therapy. We were studying Afro-Cuban dance, flamenco, ballet, and jazz. But my agenda was less around building good technique and more around healing."

She pauses. "Healing isn't the right word either, but there may not be a better one. My dancing is not so much about performance as it is about transformation."

After graduate school, Harvey's dance training shifted to what is now called conscious movement, meditation, or improvisational dance. "My intention is to build awareness with a body/mind-centering experience rather than to build choreography."

Becoming a Slam Poet

Poetry Slam, founded in 1968 by poet and construction worker Mark Smith in Chicago's Green Mill Tavern, is competitive performance poetry which requires poets to complete in three-minute rounds, relying only on their words and their bodies—props and music are not allowed.

Even though she uses the written and spoken word centrally in her art, Harvey had little formal training in writing. "Still, I have had some really good educational experiences all the way through," she explains, "like the high school poetry club and magazine, for instance. At Oxford, I did a year-long independent study project on the Beat poets."

Poetry also featured largely in her childhood home. "My uncle is a published poet, and he and my dad were always giving me poetry books. My grandma, my grandpa, and my dad are big Shakespeare fans."

Though she completed just one college class in writing and did not study writing at all in graduate school, she became the sort of "resident poet" for her graduate school dance program. "Whenever a dance needed a speaker or a writer, I was chosen. It was kind of a joke that I would be standing while everyone else was dancing." Since graduate school, she has added to her studies by completing creative writing courses at continuing education programs.

The most powerful impact on her writing and a major part of her training as a poet has come from her work in the slam poetry community. Harvey explains, "I was adamantly not a slam poet in the beginning. It was that initial jarring experience of 'It's competitive.' I wanted to be a writer. I didn't want a time limit. I didn't want my art to be scored.

"But then I went to my first slam in Los Angeles and got enamored with it. My friend wanted to go, and I said that I would go only if I could wear my pajamas. So I went in my pajamas. It was such a great group of people. I was hooked.

"The first slam team I was on was kind of scandalous in the slam world. I made both the San Jose Poetry Team and the Berkeley Slam Team. Berkeley has a better reputation, but I wanted to go with San Jose because I was really good friends with some of the San Jose members. We made semi-finals at the National Poetry Slam that year."

Harvey did participate with the Berkeley team a different year, but as performance coach. "My niche in the slam world became the performance coach. I would help the poets get the language as tight as possible, getting it in their voices and in their bodies, helping the poets to communicate their poems. I was the performance coach for the University of California-Berkeley team which took first place in the College Union Poetry Slam Invitational the year that I worked with them.

The Cantab Lounge, located in Cambridge, Massachusetts, hosts a weekly poetry open mic and slam and sends a team each year to the National Poetry Slam, the largest team poetry slam event in the world.

"Then, when I moved to Boston, I was on the Cantab team."

Successes and Failures

Harvey recalls important moments that shaped her as an artist.

"When I was an undergraduate," she says, "one of the first shows that I directed on my own was a one-woman play about the life of poet Anne Sexton that this really talented young woman had written. It was an exciting combination of stage and poetry. We earned recognition from the Kennedy Center American College Theater Festival. That felt really successful.

"But I had to collaborate with others as a professional for the first time. It was hard. I had designers and lighting people. Telling everyone how to do their jobs and then learning how to share the steering wheel was challenging. Everything turned out well, but there were some formative failures in there, too."

> Anne Sexton (1928-1974) was an American poet and playwright, whose work reflected much of her personal life, including her mental illness and struggles with depression.

For Harvey, another important learning experience came when she completed her master's thesis. "After the seminar with Peter Sellars about compassion, I was so psyched about my thesis. It got a little more metaphysical in a way that was great and took me into new research. I got to meet all these people in the Los Angeles community, people who I still work with today.

"But I abandoned some of the technique and the tangible rhetoric and politics that my committee was hoping for. My committee felt that it was a let down. My oral defense was challenging. A couple people really whipped me. One of my committee members was really, really disappointed in me."

This disappointment from a mentor helped Harvey grow more sure of herself and clearer about her goals. "Certainly," she recalls, "one part of me was just shaking and went white. It was a shock to me that this one member of my committee was so unsupportive. I felt like saying, 'Maybe you should have told me before I went down this road that you did not want me to.' Instead, I responded in a very adult and professional way. It was a growing experience of receiving intense criticism and having to defend my work, verbally right there.

"I felt really good about how everything turned out," says Harvey. "Some of what I discovered in that research are things that I am still doing today. Completing that thesis was very important to my development and having to explain it, in the end, to people I respected, helped me articulate exactly what I was doing and wanted to keep doing."

Harvey's master's thesis began a cross-cultural inquiry about concepts and theories of intuition. She explains, "What is intuition? Can it be felt in the physical body as a process? Can you witness a person experiencing an intuitive moment? Can we all agree that an intuitive moment just happened?"

She continues, "I looked at intuition as depicted in sacred art forms. I looked at yoga. I looked at an instrument played in Morocco to induce trance. I looked at intuition in conscious movement mediation. Looking at these movements, I explored how we practice intuition. I wrote a 50-60 page document and then I went into people's homes and did an intuitive experience with them. We would talk about what happened. It was transformational for me."

The Deep Conversation

As Harvey has continued to clarify her own goals as an artist, she has come to believe that the "responsibility of an artist is to express and experience something truthful and to be clear enough inside, so that we can get a sense of where the real spark is." She urges artists to "grab that spark." For her, it is from that spark that "the artistic creation and transformation" begin.

For Harvey, art is only possible if artists are authentic, if they understand themselves and are true to themselves. "As performers," she asked, "how do we feel truth? How do we know when we are being real? How do we listen deeply enough inside ourselves, so that we know we can be truthful in front of others."

For Harvey, "Being an artist and having a private practice of staying clear and focused and healthy inside are the same." She sees "artistry as a spiritual journey."

When Harvey "sits down to work" she describes herself as being "in my practice, whether that is a dance practice or a yoga practice or something that is combined. And I am listening for what is true, interesting, and vital inside. I am having what David Whyte, one of my favorite poets, would call the 'deep conversation,' the only one worth having, which is that deep conversation with self that you don't want to have but that you must have.

David Whyte is a British poet who currently lives in the Pacific Northwest of the United States. A trained naturalist, his poems reflect spirituality and a deep connection with nature.

"Having that conversation allows us to figure out a way to communicate as clearly as possible in order to transform, illuminate, or reveal some aspect of the human condition. The goal is to help others see that this is about union and community and connection. It is not about me getting up and telling my story because I am so great. It is about sharing truth. It is about saying: Here is this thing that is universally true and here is how I experienced it. Now, let's have a conversation about it."

Def Poetry Jam

The importance of the "deep conversation," of being true to herself, became clear to Harvey when she was featured on HBO's *Def Poetry Jam* in 2006, performing her poem "Spoons."

"HBO was important," says Harvey. "I was lucky to be invited to show up and to be aired. When they film you, they say that 60 percent of us will not get aired. Racially, it is really interesting. I was the only white person and one of the only women to be filmed that day. That was a big success and that opened a lot of doors. I feel really fond of and really grateful to them. My experience was really good."

The HBO experience also led Harvey to reflect on and affirm her work.

"After HBO, I asked myself, 'Okay, what am I doing? What is my work?' The poem 'Spoons' that I performed on HBO is about drug addiction and recovery—and leaving relationships that are not good for you.

"After HBO, I affirmed that my work focuses on speaking about things that are traditionally silenced, either because they are happening to people who wind up dead or they happen to people for whom these things are so traumatic that they are not given a voice.

"I started to feel a social responsibility to speak for those who can't and to push myself to become unsilent because so many are silent. I am privileged to have access to microphones and venues. It felt so real to talk about things that are not getting talked about. For me, that is trauma and violence against women, drug addiction and recovery, looking for moments of beauty and extraordinary recovery and messages of hope within that. For me, that feels socially relevant and so important."

Claiming Your Identity As an Artist

As she has developed her art practice, Harvey has learned to trust herself. She shares what she refers to as a great moment.

Vincent Van Gogh (1853-1890) was a Dutch painter, who was one of the greatest impressionist artists of the 19th century.

"I was chatting with this doctor," she recalls. "I was in this artistic personal crisis, wondering what I was doing. He pulled out a book of Van Gogh paintings, pointed to *Starry Night*, and asked, 'What do you think this guy was seeing? Trust what you see. Just don't be afraid to be what you see, be how you are experiencing the world.'

"At the time, I was feeling a lot of pressure to normalize myself and not outwardly claim an artistic identity. But he gave me permission to trust what I was seeing, trust what I was perceiving. That was an important and formative moment for me. I was able consciously to claim that the way that I am seeing the world is artistic and creative. I was able to claim my identity as an artist."

Harvey invites all artists, and especially young artists who are just beginning their careers, to experience their world fully. "As an artist, your responsibility is to live in the world and experience everything, comment on it, or change it. So keep experiencing, however that happens. Everything feeds into your art. There is no class that I have taken, no book that I have ever read that does not feed into my art."

She also urges artists to claim their identity, not to be afraid. "Declare yourself to be an artist. Claim yourself in your field. Even though it is hard to fill out applications and write 'I am an artist, I am a musician,' claim it. Even though older artists or non-artists may tell you that you have not accomplished enough yet, claim it. Be who you are. Claim your art. Push yourself to do that. Do not let anyone silence you."

You Have a Voice

Dedicated to the participants of "Between the Lines," a project in conjunction with The Attleboro Arts Museum for teens in foster care.

You have a voice.
The day you were born,
Someone shouted across an un-endable, open road:
Live! Be alive!
You have a voice!
You won't always use it, but you'll have it.
All your moments on this earth,
you'll have
a voice.

Sometimes, in the morning, or after a long night alone,
your voice will call for quiet.
It will whisper like a far away ocean,
a long ago memory of a dream.
Your voice will dream
of sunlight, of flying, of wind.
Your voice will dream of one single hummingbird,
a train over a mountain whistling
the distant sound of home.

Sometimes your voice will
blaze wildfire boom.
Your voice will

want heat and motion,
the electric snap of
a tremendous earthquake.
Your voice will be loud like
a gunshot, sharp like
the cry of a broken thing.
A piece of glass, a metal can torn in two,
a rusted bike wheel still trying
to turn.

Someday, Someone will ask you a question.
Someday Someone will ask you:
how do you feel, what do you need, who are you.
They'll say, tell me!
Tell me what makes you.
Tell me about the color of your heart.

And maybe a sound will come hell-bent and
bold from your mouth.
Or maybe a word will drip easy and soft
off a pen onto a page.
Or maybe, maybe, you'll just feel the answer
way down deep,
your own echo resounding
ancient and whole
inside your sturdy bone house of a body.

This voice will cry out, listen You!
Let me tell you about this ache of an organ inside my chest!
Let me tell you about my raging scream,
my gentle gasp,
my yes and my no,
my memories, my dreams,
my hope and my faith and
my prayer and my vision.

Let me tell you in my own words,
with my own voice,
the voice that was given to me at birth.
Planted like a seed in my belly,
trying to grow,
trying to grow strength,
trying to find a ground, a house, an ear, a moment
where I can finally,
finally be
heard.

PART II

Exploring Interrelationships Among the Arts

Introduction

Part II, Exploring Interrelationships Among the Arts, examines how the performing and fine arts build on and sustain each other. To be an artist, one must focus not only on his or her art, but must understand the relationship among the arts. The artists in the section that follows explore relationships among writing, visual arts, music, dance, digital arts, and other types of performance.

In Chapter 6, *New York Times*-bestselling novelist **Alisa Valdes-Rodriguez** explains that for her, writing is musical. The two artistic loves of Valdes-Rodriguez's life are music, especially jazz, and the written word. Her writing and her music are also deeply connected to her identity as a Latina.

Chapters 7, 8, 9, and 10 focus on the visual and sound arts. In Chapter 7, **Ellen Priest**, an abstract expressionist who paints jazz, speaks about the way that music inspires her painting. In Chapter 8, **China Blue**, a visual and sound artist, discusses the sometimes surprising intersection of sound, music, and architecture. For her, art is about inquiry and pushing boundaries; artists must challenge and expand the definition of art.

In Chapter 9, rock and roll photographer and musician **Henry Diltz** discusses the relationship between music and visual arts—as well as the ways he captures musicians on film. He also explains that his artistry has developed naturally. He considers himself "a big student of letting the universe decide." He was "open" to the "opportunities" that came along and encourages that openness in everyone.

In Chapter 10, **Lori Landay,** a new media artist, discusses the importance of examining a subject through multiple disciplines and lenses. Her work links the visual, literary, technological, and sound arts. She sees new technologies as key to fostering art in the 21st century.

For all of the artists in this section, the interactions among the arts—the ways that the visual, the musical, the written, and the performance affect each other—shed light on their understanding of the world today.

CHAPTER 6

Alisa Valdes-Rodriguez

Photo used with permission.

Writing with Music

New York Times-*bestselling novelist Alisa Valdes-Rodriguez is the author of seven novels, including the landmark* The Dirty Girls Social Club *(soon to be a prime-time TV series). She has more than one million books in print in 11 different languages.*

Valdes-Rodriguez began her career not as a writer, however, but as a musician. She is a professional saxophonist, with a Bachelor of Music from Berklee College of Music. After earning a Master of Arts in journalism from Columbia University, she moved from music to writing. For five years, she worked as a staff writer for the Boston Globe, *where she earned several Pulitzer Prize nominations and recognition as the best newspaper essayist in the nation by the SunMag organization. At the* Los Angeles Times, *she reported on the pop music industry. There, she won an award for feature-writing from the American Society of Sunday Newspaper Editors.*

Writing novels full time since 2001, Valdes-Rodriguez has had tremendous success. Entertainment Weekly *named her a breakout literary star, and* Latina *magazine named her a Woman of the Year.* Hispanic Business *magazine has twice named her among the 100 most influential Hispanics in the nation. And* Time *magazine has named her one of the 25 most influential Hispanics in America, alongside George Lopez, Bill Richardson, Jennifer Lopez, and others.*

Valdes-Rodriguez' influence and appeal were further reflected in her entry into young adult crossover literature with her planned trilogy, The Kindred.

In this chapter, Valdes-Rodriguez explores the relationship between music and writing. In fact, for Valdes-Rodriguez, her understanding of music makes writing possible.

For Alisa Valdes-Rodriguez, writing is musical. It helps her bridge the two artistic loves of her life—music and the written word. Writing also allows her to portray the diversity of the Latino population in popular music and literature. Her writing, her music, her artistry, are deeply connected to her identity as a Latina.

Valdes-Rodriguez likens her writing to jazz improvisation. "The whole concept of jazz improvisation is that you spend a lot of time in a practice room getting very familiar with chord changes and the kind of scales and patterns that you can play over those changes. You memorize those different shapes and patterns—licks or whatever you call them—so that when the time comes and you get up to improvise, you have this incredible arsenal of memorized prepared stuff that is in your muscle memory and in your hands.

"A lot of people who don't know this think, 'Oh, jazz. People get up and just play random notes.' But this is not the case. They are not just playing random notes. They are spontaneously composing. And someone like a Charlie Parker or a John Coltrane, their spontaneous compositions were very complicated and brilliant. These guys were able to do this in the instant because they were prepared."

Valdes-Rodriguez explains that she writes books the way she would prepare for a concert. "I have a soundtrack for each of my characters." Her characters come alive to her through her understanding of the kind of music they would put on their iPod. She also has a "soundtrack for the overall shape and tone of the book."

She explains, "If the book is in three parts, and the first part is 'life as usual,' which is the typical story track, the second part is 'conflict and chaos,' and the third part is 'resolving the conflict and happy ending,' I'll have on my iPod a playlist for each part. And I love to write in my mind, without sitting down somewhere. I do a lot of writing while walking, or on rollerblades, or hiking, or bike riding, or while driving in my car. And I will listen to that soundtrack. I will get the gut feeling of the shape and color and tone of the story and of the personality and mood of the characters, how they think and how their voice should be.

"Then, when I sit down to write, everything is in place in exactly the same way that memorizing chord changes and the licks I could improvise would be in my head before I would set foot on the stage as a saxophone player.

"There is also some method acting in my writing," says Valdes-Rodriguez. "My first book, for instance, was written from six points of view. Before I would sit down and write the character of 'Elizabeth,' I would try to talk like her and walk like her. I would go to the grocery store and behave the way she would. This could be annoying if you were my friend and shopping with me. But that is how I do it. That seemed very musical to me. It was like getting inside of a song. You had to get into that space."

As Valdes-Rodriguez reflects on her writing method, she recalls, "There are stories about Coltrane on the road and his band mates would say, 'We're going to go shopping. Why don't you join us?' He would refuse and would stay in the room, practicing. He would be playing one lick, two bars long, with the metronome moving really slowly. They would come back at noon, and he would have moved the metronome up a few beats, so it was a little faster but he was still playing the same lick.

"They would say, 'We're going to lunch now' and he would say, 'No, no, I'm busy.'

"They would return at six o'clock and he would still be there, playing that same lick, but now at lightning speed. And he would never forget it. So he had this kind of intensity of focus. And I have that for writing.

"I am not saying I am as good a writer as Coltrane was a player, but that is the closest I have come in descriptions of creativity, reading that he was focused and was in his own world. That is how I write."

Writing and Music

Valdes-Rodriguez's love of writing and of music grew together and were always equally strong. "I wrote my first short story when I was nine years old, and that is the same year that I started to play the saxophone. My parents are both writers. My mom—she works as a magazine copy-editor now and is a poet and a novelist—she never really sends out her work but she writes a lot. My dad is an academic and writes scholarly pieces.

"I remember being three or four years old and pretending that I could write because I thought writing was very cool. I grew up with a lot of reading and writing. I just loved it.

"And I grew up with a lot of music, too. We lived in New Orleans for three years. My parents loved Jazzfest, which was just starting at that time. They used to drag my brother and me to that. They were sort of hippie parents and they used to humiliate us by doing interpretive dancing, while my brother and I covered our eyes and pretended not to know them." She laughs.

"But, in retrospect, this had a big influence on me, being able to go to a lot of concerts and outdoor events and see people enjoy jazz. They were not necessarily dissecting it and trying to figure it out, but were just dancing to it and having fun. I always thought those things were cool and I feel lucky that I had the kind of parents where I could say I want to be a musician or a writer and they said, 'That's fantastic.' I know a lot of people whose parents have said, 'Well, why don't you be a dentist and then you can still play on the side?'"

In high school in Albuquerque, New Mexico, Valdes-Rodriguez played in the band and wrote for the school literary journal. "It was," she says, "always a question of which I wanted to do more—write or play." When her parents divorced, her mother moved back to New Orleans and her father stayed in New Mexico. Valdes-Rodriguez, living with her mother, enrolled in the New Orleans Center for Creative Arts, the performing arts high school. She was the first student in the school's history to complete a dual track of creative writing and jazz.

"For me," she says, "writing and music were always the same thing. I see language as very musical. I learned writing through reading and reading out loud. I love to read out loud and I love to listen to audio books. I guess the musical parallel would be learning it by ear.

"Music was harder for me than writing. I felt that I had to work harder to achieve the same level of success. I thought writing was easy and that everyone could write. So, even though I had teachers and family members saying 'You are really good at writing—that is what you should do'—I thought, everyone does that. That's so boring. It's not cool. As a writer, you are not in front of a crowd. You are not the center of attention. I wanted to be on stage and I wanted to perform."

This desire led Valdes-Rodriguez to Berklee College of Music. "I came with a bunch of blank notebooks," she says, "and I spent all my free time writing poems. I was in a poetry group."

One of her most important memories at Berklee is not of sharing her music with fellow students, but of sharing her poetry. One day, she and her roommate, the now successful saxophonist Mindi Abair, threw a party. Jazz guitarist Kurt Rosenwinkel, also a student with Valdes-Rodriguez, attended. "None of these people were stars yet," says Valdes-Rodriguez. "We were all students together but, even then, I knew that those two would be successful.

"Kurt was looking around my room and he found my notebooks. And I said, 'Don't look at those,' but he picked one up. I remember it was one with a yellow cover. Kurt sat down cross-legged on the floor, and instead of participating in the party, he spent the rest of the night reading my poems and telling me how great they were. This was a defining moment for me.

"Kurt was an awesome player then and I sort of worshipped him. We played in a band together. I knew he was supportive of my playing, but he never got the look on his face from my playing that he got that night when he read my writing. That was a moment when I thought, as an artist, I probably am better at writing than at music, because even Kurt Rosenwinkel is impressed."

After graduating from Berklee, Valdes-Rodriguez went to New York and worked as a musician, playing weddings and playing for a cruise ship. She also began an unpaid internship at *The Village Voice*. As she explains, "I had always nurtured both writing and music, and I loved both. I could never really decide which I wanted to focus on. My internship at the *Voice Literary Supplement* piqued my interest in the fiction world and the world of books. It was so refreshing for me. It was wonderful to be around people who understood what I was talking about, who were reading books, who had ideas, and who respected me. I felt empowered in that world and I wanted to stay in it. I thought I would love to get paid to do this kind of work.

"I remember telling my dad that I was thinking of going on to earn a master's in journalism and he said, 'Well, you know the best journalism school in the world is at Columbia University in New York. Why don't you apply?' I was insecure and I thought, 'I will never get in there. It's an ivy-league school. Why would they want me?' But he said, 'Give it a shot.' Everyone should have a dad like that. He was right."

Valdes-Rodriguez explains that Columbia does not offer an under-graduate degree in journalism because the school wants its students to have an expertise in another area before they become journalists. "The fact that I had gone to Berklee and had a music degree, and had even written some music reviews for the *Boston Globe* was a benefit to me."

A Reporter's Life

After Columbia, Valdes-Rodriguez joined the staff of the *Boston Globe* as a features writer. She had, as she describes it, "a lot of free reign" to write long-form features, pieces that would take up three broad sheet pages, long by newspaper standards. The articles were less journalism than they were creative nonfiction, she explains. "I would live with mi-grant farm workers in western Massachusetts for a week and write about that experience, or I would follow for weeks an ill child who was being given a trip by the Make-a-Wish Foundation. Instead of doing the typical short story—sick child is given trip—the *Globe* allowed me to present the life of the child in print. I would go with him to chemo, interview him and his family, and report on this horrible and painful stuff."

Valdes-Rodriguez credits being allowed to be experimental at the *Boston Globe* with helping her develop as a fiction writer. A first-person essay that she wrote about a trip she took to Cuba, entitled "Daughter of Cuba," won the national SunMag Contest, a competition for best essay judged by the editors of the all the papers that carry the Sunday Magazine insert.

For Valdes-Rodriguez, "being a journalist is almost like constant graduate school because you are always learning things. You are given permission to go and ask people questions that you would never ask them normally, and you are in situations where you would never be. As a fiction writer later, I have been able to draw on this."

She recalls reporting on a jetliner that crashed in Halifax. The crash happened at night, and everyone died on the plane. She had to pick up and go at a moment's notice. She recalls, "Flying into the air space within three hours of this horrible crash, I felt the energy of all these lost souls. It was something that I could not have ever imagined."

For Valdes-Rodriguez, "the horrible stuff made me courageous and made me a better writer." Still, Valdes-Rodriguez missed music. She was writing features for the *Boston Globe* and would occasionally cover music stories. When she saw that the *Los Angeles Times* had an opening for a pop music writer, covering the Latin music industry, she was very excited.

"I had pushed a lot at the *Globe* for fairness in their coverage of mu-sic. They would cover a lot of jazz, which is fine. But there would be these huge shows of Latin artists at Boston's Wonderland Ballroom—people like Marc Anthony, before anyone knew who he was, or La India, or Jerry Rivera—and, there would be no coverage. There would be 4,000 people, and the *Globe* didn't even know that these artists existed. I pushed a lot to increase coverage. The editors would say, 'Hispanics are not reading the paper' and I would say, 'Well, maybe you are not writing anything that is of interest to them.'"

Wonderland Ballroom is an entertainment complex that describes itself as *"Boston's only venue specializing in concerts featuring the world's top performers from Reggae, Latin, Brazilian, hard rock, and more."*

Marc Anthony (1968-) is a musician, singer-songwriter, and actor. Anthony is the top selling tropical salsa artist of all time and the first solo salsa act ever to sell out Madison Square Garden. The five-time Grammy winner has sold more than thirty million albums worldwide.

La India (1969-), known also as "La Princesa de la Salsa," has released eight albums including *Jazzin' with Tito Puente*. She has been nominated for both Grammy and Latin Grammy awards.

Jerry Rivera (1973-) is a Puerto Rican salsa singer. He has released seventeen albums in twenty years and has had dozens of singles on *Billboard*'s Hot Latin chart.

When the *Los Angeles Times* created its Latino initiative, an effort to hire reporters to do exactly what she was trying to do at the *Globe*, Valdes-Rodriguez applied. "When I learned that one of the positions was dedicated to covering Latin pop music, I was the first to raise my hand. I got the job, and that was really fun." This was her chance to join together her passions for music and writing with her deep commitment to challenging Latino stereotypes and promoting information about the Latino population in the United States.

Latin Identity

For Valdes-Rodriguez, her identity as a Latina is very much connected to her work as an artist. "My fiction," she explains, "focuses on the diversity of the Latin population in the United States, that this is not a one-size-fits-all population. That awareness is not something that I always had. I learned that.

"In Boston, where most of the Latin population is Puerto Rican and Dominican, the music that I knew as Latin was merengue and salsa. When I went to Los Angeles, my first assignment was to cover a singer named Juan Gabriel in a rodeo arena in Pico Rivera. I had never heard of him. Yet, there he was, with a cape and patent leather shoes, and 10,000 people watching. Or the Staples Center would be sold out for singers I did not know, who came out on horseback and wearing giant sombreros. This was Mexican music that I had never paid attention to. That was really eye-opening for me, that this population that is mostly presented in the media as impoverished is very different in real life. That Mexico has hugely wealthy superstars was surprising and fascinating for me.

"By virtue of my last name, editors assumed I would know this whole Latin world, and I didn't know it at all, but I learned. I feel like I should have an honorary degree in Latin culture or Latin studies for all

Juan Gabriel (1950-) is a Mexican singer and songwriter who has written and recorded hundreds of songs. His style incorporates Mexican ranchera, mariachi, and pop music. In 1996, he was inducted into Billboard magazine's Latin Music Hall of Fame in 1996.

that I learned. It was very humbling and it has been very useful for me.

"At the time I was in Los Angeles, the top three FM radio stations played Mexican regional music, but you wouldn't know it to look at the paper. I was able to change that."

Her interest in representing a diverse Latin culture led Valdes-Rodriguez from journalism to fiction. She explains, "I always wanted to write fiction. Finally, I found an agent who said to me, 'You know, publishing is looking for a Latina Terry McMillan, someone who is going to write about middle-class, assimilated, successful Latinas in the U.S. That is an untapped literary market.'

"I sat with that idea for about a year," says Valdes-Rodriguez. "Under the Latin umbrella, you have incredible diversity in the people and the music. You can go to a club. They will put the merengue on, and all the Dominicans get up

Terry McMillan (1951-) is a *New York Times*-bestselling author of several novels including *Mama, Waiting to Exhale, How Stella Got Her Groove Back, Disappearing Acts, A Day Late and a Dollar Short, The Interruption of Everything*, and *Getting to Happy*. Her protagonists are, African-American professional women.

and dance. And then the salsa comes on, and all the Puerto Ricans get up and dance. So I had to think about how I could write in a way that appealed to a wide diversity of people. When I finally figured out how I thought I would do it, I quit my job and I said, 'Well, I am going to go and try this thing and see if it works.' And so, I became a novelist."

Valdes-Rodriguez wants her books to represent a population—smart, professional, sophisticated Latin women—that is underrepresented in fiction and to show the diversity of her culture. With her first novel, *The Dirty Girls Social Club*, she strove "to write a book about Latinas that shows, by the time people got to the end of the book, that there is really no such thing as a 'Latina.' Readers see the diversity of characters who fit the definition. You have a Black person. You have a blonde person of Austrian descent. There is a Jewish person, a pagan, a Catholic. I wanted to show that no one is predictable by virtue of belonging to a group. That very notion offends me."

She explains, "I write what I think are universal stories. With my first book, the stories were about domestic violence and coping with that for one character; coming out of the closet for another character; one of the characters is dealing with her cheating fiancé; she also has bulimia.

I wanted to put those universal things in there. And it works in a way. I have all kinds of readers."

Still, says Valdes-Rodriguez, "the majority of my readers are Hispanic women. I do try to write for them, too, something that they will like. I have met so many of them, and they come up in tears, saying that this is the first time that they think they have seen themselves in the characters in books. I am proud of that and don't want them to lose that."

Artistic Goals

Valdes-Rodriguez knows that her goals as an artist have changed as she has gotten older. She is now less concerned about herself and more concerned with the message she conveys.

"When I was younger," she explains, "I wanted the focus to be on me. When I was playing saxophone, I wanted it to be about me. Even in early writing, for the *Globe*, I wanted everyone to admire my facility with language. The older I get, that is less important to me. I want to entertain people and I want to help them. I want to make people's lives better. Creatively, that is why I write happy endings, and books that are uplifting and fun and aspirational, something that you would want to happen to you, almost fantasy."

Valdes-Rodriguez has also learned the importance of perseverance.

"The difference between the people who make it and the people who don't," she says, "isn't always a matter of talent but is a matter of sticking with it. You have got to develop a thick skin. You cannot let rejection stop you because we all get rejected. You have to start with the assumption that the people who reject you don't know what they are talking about. And you have to just keep pushing and be true to your vision of who you are. It doesn't matter what genre you are in. Sometimes it takes a while to get the recognition you deserve, but if you are sincere and keep at it, it will come."

She explains that she has known "in a psychic way since I was in the sixth grade that I would be a published novelist. I know it sounds crazy, but I have known this."

When she quit her fulltime job as a reporter in order to write her own novels, she was unafraid. "There was never any fear," she says. "It was an impatience that I felt. My soul told me that I had to leave and do this thing. I had to write."

CHAPTER 7

Ellen Priest

Photo used with permission.

Seeing the World

Ellen Priest is a contemporary painter whose solo exhibitions have been held at the Delaware Division of the Arts (2010); the Philip and Muriel Berman Museum of Art in Collegeville, Pennsylvania (2007); the DuPont Clifford Brown Jazz Festival in conjunction with the Carspecken-Scott Gallery in Wilmington, Delaware (2006); and the Alva Gallery in New London, Connecticut (2004); among other locations.

In February 2009, Priest and composer Edward Simon presented "Composing the 'Venezuelan Suite': The Music and The Painting" as part of the Department of Music Colloquium Series at New York University. Paintings from the "Venezuelan Suite" were also exhibited at the Delaware Center for the Contemporary Arts 2010 Show "SPECTRUM: Contemporary Color Abstraction."

Priest serves as a part-time faculty member at the Professional Institute for Educators at the University of the Arts in Philadelphia, and received Pollock-Krasner Foundation Grants in both 2001 and 2007.

Priest earned a Bachelor of Arts in Government from Lawrence University in Wisconsin and a Master of Divinity from Yale Divinity School. At Yale, she focused on Christianity and the Visual Arts, completing an interdisciplinary program in collaboration with the University's School of Art.

Priest also developed a studio art program for children called Eyeball It. This at-home program for elementary school children consists of discreet art projects based upon natural patterns for the growth of visual and spatial intelligence.

In this chapter, Priest speaks about the relationship among the arts and the ways that, for her, music inspires painting.

Ellen Priest, a visual artist, primarily in the abstract expressionist style, takes jazz as her subject matter and creates paintings that move. As she puts it, "My paintings are constructed from superimposed layers of paper—the back layer opaque watercolor paper, the front layers translucent vellum—each with drawing, color, and more recently, collage. One sees a painting through a painting."

Movement motivates her. "That's what grabbed my imagination nearly thirty years ago when I saw

Abstract expressionism is a style of painting in which artists focus on showing emotions rather than representing images. The style is characterized by the rapid application of paint to large canvases. Some artists use large brushes; some drip or throw paint. The style may give the appearance of accident but is usually highly planned. Some of the best-known artists in this style include Mark Rothko (American, 1903-1970), Willem De Kooning (Dutch-American, 1904-1997), Jackson Pollock (American, 1912-1956), and Helen Frankenthaler (American, 1928-).

[Paul] Cezanne's late watercolors and oils at the Museum of Modern Art's 1977 exhibition, 'Cezanne: The Late Works,'" she explains. "I had never seen paintings that moved so magically between two- and three-dimensionality. Then there was the glorious translucence. I felt it was an artistic avenue laid out by Cezanne's work and not well explored by his successors. To me, Cezanne's late paintings were the work of a man who saw the physical world in color densities—not solids and spaces—and all of it was dynamic. From his work, I recognized my own vision over the next several years."

Paul Cezanne (1839-1906) was a French post-Impressionist painter whose work is thought to provide a bridge between Impressionism and modern styles, such as Cubism.

Jazz: Edward Simone's Venezuelan Suite #10. Oil, flashe, and MSA gel on collaged paper. 42" x 42", 2006.

Studies for Jazz: Edward Simone's Venezuelan Suite #10. Oil, flashe, and MSA gel on collaged paper. 42" x 42", 2006.

Priest remakes abstract expressionism in her own image, embracing a distinctive methodology in order to convey what is most important to her. An athlete, Priest believes that her athleticism is clear in her work, and that athletic people are often attracted to her paintings.

As she explains, "The rough, blunt emotions and compositional athleticism of abstract expressionism grab me.

"I recently realized how physical my work is," says Priest. "It is a relief surface with big collage pieces on it. Up close it is an object but also has the illusion of movement, and I want that. The fact that I understand physical movement so well comes through my work. Throughout college and graduate school, I have done a lot of modern dance. Though not well," she laughs.

"I skate and ride my bicycle. I swim and I walk a lot. I water skied growing up. I have always done weight and balance sports—all the things where you throw your weight. Skiing is a great example: You throw your weight out of balance in order to maintain your balance. That has really been my understanding of movement: being able to throw my body. There is a sense of risk, an understanding of balance and motion that is different from if you are standing up in place. This is why movement in my paintings at the scale that they are—which is really a human scale—is believable.

"Someone once asked me if I thought I could do the work that I do if I were not athletic. I don't know. I don't think so. It is not like I am a stellar athlete. I love doing physical things. For me, there is a joy in motion. It feels really alive to me. And this is part of my work."

Defining Her Own Style

Asked to define her work, Priest explains that it is "an outgrowth of abstract expressionism. The brush studies that I do are straight abstract expressionism. One, two minute brush studies. The paintings—I don't know if I should be calling them paintings anymore—are really painted collages or painted relief constructions. They are as much low-relief sculpture with paint as they are paintings.

"I still consider them paintings, because the imagery is all generated by paint. The imagery all comes from these brush studies, and the medium I use is paint—paint, paper, and glue. They are definitely on the border between object and illusion. That is very important to me.

"I want my artwork to capture that tension in our lives between what is physical and tangible and what isn't—and how the intangible stays with us. Things can make us happy and sad years after we have physically experienced them. So it is that interface and that constant back and forth between the physical and the non-physical that I try to get to happen in the work itself."

Priest explains why jazz is the subject that helps her capture this tension: "Jazz evokes in me what I would like to evoke in the people who view my work. There must be some fit between the spaces and rhythms in jazz and all of its multicultural roots in Africa and Latin America that matches the spaces that have meaning to me."

As she continues to analyze this, she points to aspects of herself and her work that she does not yet understand. "We are right up against the part of me that is opaque to me. There is something about the spaces and structure of jazz that matches whatever in me that relates to me. There was never any decision in me. I went from not using music at all straight to jazz. There was never a consideration of other music or even a decision to use music as a subject matter. This was just the fit.

"In the early 1990s, when I switched to jazz, I tried to get to the rhythm structure without using a grid. Whenever I am in a transition with my art, I do something that I call stupidly literal—it is so concrete and literal—because thinking about it is never the same as having it physically in front of me. So I thought, well, if the bass and drums are keeping this together and they are the rhythmic bottom line of a lot of jazz, why don't I try making the bottom layer of my paintings structured according to the rhythm in the piece. I took a form from the front layer and started repeating it, rotating it, according to the beats in the back layer, and it worked. To my great surprise, it was like, 'Damn, this worked.' I tried a couple of other things before, and they were interesting but they did not cut it.

"My pieces are composed by laying out on the floor a whole bunch of brush studies and choreographing them, moving them around, until I get groups of three or four that I know are going to have the dynamic that I am looking for when they are superimposed on each other.

"Then to make the piece cohere, I use a form that I hear from the front layer, tilted and repeated on the back layer. I paint into the back layer in a way I would not paint in the front layer. I flip positive and negative. I make positive and negative interchangeable. Then I build in front of that in the other layers. Color is what helps me establish the position of form in the space moving forward. Color is how I get the space in front and behind the picture plane.

"The way I build my paintings—it is all about looking. So working with musicians, I guess it is a funny blend. I am listening, but my own imagination is so visual that the music builds spaces and color relationships in my head. I hear the music very spatially."

She continues, "I know the kind of spaces I 'see' intuitively are not real world, realist spaces. They move differently. So I paint gestural abstraction, with Cezanne always in the back of my mind."

Education

Priest's journey to artistry is as unique as her paintings. "I came of age in the Vietnam era," says Priest. "I had a tough, no-roses view of the world and my place in it—and a big heart. These were not easy to reconcile."

She came to art via Yale Divinity School. It was a journey that her heart directed, and one that she could not resist, despite the social pressure to do so.

She explains, "If you were a bright kid growing up in Duluth, Minnesota in the 1950s and 1960s, as I was, art was not an option. Not really. I had no art classes between second grade and my senior year in college. Because if you had the ability to be a lawyer or a doctor, you did that, not art.

"Of course, for women at that point, doctoring and lawyering were not even really options—and that is a separate thing I want to talk about, how my dad gave me permission to do and be anything.

"But especially for a girl growing up in that era, art was for the 'dumb' kids, for those who could not 'handle' the real subjects at school. If you could handle Latin and calculus, that is where you were put. There was no understanding of visual intelligence or emotional intelligence. In school, I studied languages and sciences but not art."

Priest returns to the subject of her father. She remembers that even though choices were limited for women while she was growing up, she was extremely fortunate to have a father who expected that she pursue a profession. "My Dad and I were very close. He died when I was nineteen. My Dad said something to me when I was fourteen that has shaped my life. Realizing that I was worried about what everyone thought of me, he sat me down and said, 'Ellen, you have to do what makes you happy.' And he meant long range and short range because he knew that I was not going to take it in some kind of silly way. 'You have to do what makes you happy and if that is digging ditches, then you go dig ditches.' My paintings are my ditches. It just took a while for me to figure that out."

For more about visual intelligence, see the work of Donald Hoffman, Professor of Logic and Philosophy of Science, University of California, Davis. Hoffman's groundbreaking work, *Visual Intelligence: How We Create What We See* (1998), explains: "Vision is not merely a matter of passive perception, it is an intelligent process of active construction."

For more about emotional intelligence, see Daniel Goleman's *Emotional Intelligence: Why It Can Matter More than IQ* (1995). This *New York Times* bestseller, based on brain and behavioral research, argues "emotional intelligence"—including self-awareness, altruism, empathy, and the ability to love—is the strongest indicator of human success.

Priest arrived at her senior year at Lawrence University as a government major. Just as she was about to begin her honors thesis, her history professor, noticing that she was struggling, asked her if this was her passion, if working on this thesis was how she wanted to spend her last year of college.

Priest recalls him saying, "'Ellen, is this really worth a year of your life to you?' I did not even have to hesitate. I said, 'No,' and he said, 'Then you should not be writing an honors thesis." Priest skipped the honors thesis, completed an urban studies program in Washington, D.C., and took courses in ceramics and sculpture.

She says, "I was purely going by what was attracting me, pulling me, rather than by someone else's 'oughts.' It wasn't that I was not interested in the other stuff. I was but it did not grab me by the gut." Art grabbed her, yet she still continued to push it away, not realizing that this would, ultimately, become not just her career, but her calling—who she was—and is: an artist.

Priest took a year off between college and graduate school. "I wasn't sure what I wanted to do," she recalls. This was 1972 and 1973. The country was in a major recession and Priest's class was really the first with a large number of college graduates who were not able to find jobs.

"I was in Boston," she recalls, "because I just wanted to be in another part of the country. I found a ceramics studio and started taking classes, and it still never occurred to me to do anything serious with it. Plus, I wanted to go to Divinity School. I wasn't sure about the ministry, but I wanted to go in that direction for more education."

At Yale, while focusing on divinity, Priest took a sculpture class and realized that she felt "more and more at home." She created her own program: She completed all the requirements for the Master of Divinity and took all of her electives in art and art history. She explains, "So I took drawing and color and all that stuff, finished my MDiv and took the Presbyterian exam; I did all the ordination exams and preached the sermons, and in the meantime, I realized that there was such a thing as visual intelligence. No one was talking about it yet, but I knew there was. I knew that is where I was at home. But what I was going to do with it at that time, I was not sure."

One friend, artist Gerry Bergstein, a faculty member at the School of the Museum of Fine Arts, Boston, was pivotal in her development, supporting her as she began her focus on abstraction and as she realized, "that I had to do this myself.

"I can't imagine how many hours I spent at the Museum of Modern Art, just staring at things until I understood them, reading like crazy. I was reading artists' biographies, artists' writing about their own work, their teaching, and I got an education that way."

This self-education, and the journey into art through other study, helped her shape her goals and define her purpose. She has no regrets, but she does acknowledge a lack in her education: "I lack what one does in art school, just drawing the figure and doing the exercises. I draw reasonably well but I don't draw as well as I would like to. My abstract drawing has gotten stronger over the years." Her ability to express her emotions and thoughts, to evoke a mood in the viewer without creating a realistic image, has improved. "I did not even realize that there was such a thing as abstract drawing at first," she adds. "But I can see that there is, because I can see it in my work, and I can see my development."

Spirituality and Art

Somewhere in her late 20s, says Priest, she realized abstract drawing is what drives her to get up in the morning. "This is it," she says. "This is where the rubber hits the road.

"When I was at Yale, I had the opportunity to do a week-long Ignatian retreat with a Jesuit spiritual director with whom one of my professors also took retreats. An Ignatian retreat is based on the spiritual exercises of Ignatius of Loyola. It is a week of prayer and silence, and you meet with your spiritual director once a week.

"The retreat does not focus on theology so much as prayer and spiritual life. This approach is something that I have followed all the way," says Priest. "Over the next few years I did three retreats, and my painting was built into them." The director, someone with whom Priest still works, realized the deep connection between her art and her spirituality. He encouraged her to paint while she was at the retreats. Priest became "intellectually, aesthetically, emotionally, and spiritually connected in my art."

She considers herself a spiritual person, yet she hesitates to discuss this. "I don't want my work to be categorized as religious art, because it is just art. Whatever it says to people, it just says. I think it is too easy to dismiss my work if it is pigeon-holed as religious art. My work is not religious art. It is an outgrowth of abstract expressionism and my subject matter is jazz."

Still, for Priest, it was her spirituality that gave her the push she needed to commit her life to artistry and, as she puts it, "to go way out on a limb with the work and just to take risk after risk after risk after risk. Some people don't need a religious motivation for that. I needed that kind of grounding."

Her spirituality also helped her survive challenging times. "You have to realize," she says, "that for fifteen years I did not show at all and not because I wasn't trying to. My work has been out of fashion. Every year there is a different way that it is out of fashion. It is like hemlines. That used to really matter to me. At this point, my style is formed, and I have had some success, finally.

"But there was a long time that I was out on a limb in the dark. There is no question that my spiritual life helped me to survive that and maintain a sense of direction and purpose and clarity about where I was going and what I was doing.

"I want my work to evoke joy and energy in my viewers. It can be in a secular way or it can be seen as having a religious grounding. But the minute you say spiritual life or sacred, people can have so much baggage about that. You know, the work is going to say to you what you want it say. Take it where you want. I have no desire to hit you over the head with it."

Her spirituality helps Priest understand herself. It also helps her reflect very deliberately about who she is and how her identity affects her work. She attributes her self-reflective nature, in part, to her generation. "My generation tends to be always serious and heavy. I think that is a product of the Vietnam era, and I don't think we have ever really shaken it. Not that we can't have fun, but we can't shake it."

She also attributes her self-reflective nature to her personality and how it was affected by divinity school, which taught her how to be very clear about one's purpose and one's thinking. "Yale really taught me to think," Priest explains. "When you are doing theology all the time, Biblical history, all this sort of stuff, at a place like Yale, or a really top-notch school, you can't have oatmeal in your brain.

"I think I've always been a person who has thought about what I was doing and why I was doing it—maybe to a fault—but with the art-work, the great thing about it, is that I can really get engrossed in it.

"The intellectual side of my art is helpful, too, because it gives me purpose and direction, so that my work does not just wander. This is important for abstraction. I can't speak for realism, but for abstraction, it is so easy to wander and to end up just repeating yourself."

Mentors: Internalizing Your Teachers

For Priest, a mentor was incredibly influential in determining her artistic direction and in shaping the kinds of questions that she asks herself about her work and about her life. At Yale, she studied with John W. Cook, whose field is religion and the arts. He led her to read Rudolf Arnheim's *Art and Visual Perception* and Susanne Langer's *Feeling and Form*. From these readings, Priest began to investigate the ways that art carries meaning. "Langer helped me understand that in art, there is the subject—in my case, it is jazz, but it might be a landscape or a love affair or whatever. Then there is the technical part—the medium, all that stuff; then there is composition—how everything is arranged. All the pieces of the puzzle come together, and this results in movement. I am grossly oversimplifying, but this helped me understand my work.

Rudolf Arnheim (1904-2007) was an art theorist and perceptual psychologist, whose work *Art and Visual Perception: A Psychology of the Creative Eye* (1954) redefined the visual process in psychological terms. He argues that the human eye organizes visual material according to psychological premises.

"Movement is the carrier of meaning in art. And that could be the flow of the narrative in a play or the flow of a visual thing. In my work, the movement is imaginary. It is the movement that forms in the piece, the colors that swell and shift. From both Arnheim and Langer, I learned that we are using cues to read art and to get around in the world, and that is true whether you are looking at an Egyptian wall, or Goya, or Jackson Pollock. Your eyes are using those same tools to judge space, to judge what it is in front and behind, to judge bigger and smaller, to judge direction. Movement in visual art is what carries the punch.

Susanne Langer (1895-1985) was one of the first women to be recognized as a major American philosopher and scholar. She is best known for *Philosophy in a New Key: A Study in the Symbolism of Reason, Rite, and Art* (1941). She argues that symbolism is a key to expression, that human beings create symbols, see one thing in terms of another, in order to understand their world. Her 1953 book, *Feeling and Form: A Theory of Art*, applies this philosophy to art—exploring what art is, how it works, why it moves us, and how we create it.

"After reading Arnheim, I understood that simple things like a picture plane, which artists talk about as a flat, empty space, the physical surface—transforms. The minute you work with that as art and let your imagination go—that surface has the ability to move in your imagination. What we read in a piece of art depends on our own understanding—of weight, balance, gravity, and more—whether our language reads right to left, up to down, whatever.

"For example," continues Priest, "take a piece of art the size of one of my paintings, 42 inches x 42 inches, and paint it yellow and stick a dot in the middle. It will feel like it is dropping because of gravity. To make it look like the dot is in the middle you have to put it above the middle. That is Arnheim. Artists know this. Some of this is intuitive but much is learned.

"It is like working with the edge of the picture plane. We never know what to do with the edge. I find this in my students, whether they are children or adults. They don't know what to do with the edge, whether to let the picture go off. They either want to push things into the picture or pull them out. The edge is where the imaginary world of the picture plane meets reality. So anything that I put in front of the edge is going to pop way forward. All that dynamic understanding of the visuals of art—that is all Arnheim.

"I read these two people early in my life as an artist, and it has shaped everything I have done. It has shaped my teaching. It has shaped my ability to critique my own work. It has shaped my thinking."

Advice to Young Artists

Priest teaches at the University of the Arts in Philadelphia. She offers this advice: "As students, you are reacting to problems, issues, and solutions that have been set up or offered by professors. Even though you do your own work in graduate school, you are still reacting to the pushes and pulls of faculty. It is not until you are out of school—and I have seen this so many times—that you kind of get the picture that you have to figure out what is important to you. You need to define your own issues and artistic problems and find your own voice.

"You have to figure out who you are and will be," says Priest. "I look at my own idiosyncratic background at this point, and I think that one of the strengths of my work is that I have consciously chosen at many points along the way not to try to be someone other than who I am. As if I could choose that," she adds, "but we often have the illusion that we could.

"Stripping away the overlay of other people's biases and prejudices and whatever else, stripping all that away has only helped me and only helped my work."

This stripping away is also extremely useful "for when I get stuck, says Priest. When everything is rolling, this is not a problem. But when it is not rolling, then this understanding of my purpose and myself, helps me: How do I ask the questions to get me unstuck.

"This is one of the things that is most important to me, and what I would say to young or aspiring artists is: Really learn the questions to ask yourself and your work when it is not flowing. At school, your teachers and mentors are asking you these questions all the time. Or you hear these questions from your classmates.

"That ability to ask yourself questions should always be in the back of your mind. It is something you learn at school and need to take with you after you graduate. When you don't need it, when you are operating intuitively, you go, but, inevitably, there are moments—small moments in the process of a work, or large moments over the years—when it does not just flow." Knowing yourself, explains Priest, means you can ask yourself the questions that need to be explored, and this will foster your success.

For Priest, success comes, of course, from critical recognition of her work, sales, grants, and exhibitions. But, more important, it comes from her personal assessment. "Have I created artwork that satisfies my largest goals? This is the success that allows me to look myself in the eye after nearly thirty years in the studio and feel happy. This is also the one that keeps shifting, and moving farther out ahead of me as the work continues to grow."

This is the kind of success she wishes for all artists.

CHAPTER 8

China Blue

Photo used with permission.

Listening to and Recording the World

China Blue, a visual and sound artist, was the first person to record the Eiffel Tower in Paris, France. She took a microphone to the Tower and recorded the sounds that the structure makes. She is also a two-time recipient of a NASA and Rhode Island Space Grant for work done recording NASA's Vertical Gun at Moffett Field, California.

Her work has been shown in galleries and non-profit spaces in Finland, Sweden, France, and the United States. She was the U.S. representative at OPEN XI, Venice, Italy, an exhibition held in conjunction with the Architecture Biennale, and was the featured artist for the 2006 annual meeting of the Acoustical Society of America.

China Blue earned a Bachelor of Fine Arts from California College of the Arts and a Master of Fine Arts from Hunter College. She has been an adjunct faculty member and fellow at Brown University. Her most recent work is based on the emergence of new biological forms from obsolescent technology.

In this chapter, China Blue discusses the need for artists to challenge and expand definitions of art.

China Blue sits in her home studio, a cup of tea in her hands. The sun streams in, a fat cat stretches before her, a beautiful white orchid blooms on her table, and small sculptures and images of the Eiffel Tower clutter the shelves behind her. Clearly, she is comfortable in her own space.

Likewise, China Blue is comfortable in her art. For her, art is about inquiry and about pushing boundaries. She tries to ask and answer the questions she has about the world through her artistic work.

"A lot of people," China Blue says, "have basic skill sets. They know how to shape things to make sculptures and paint images that they develop into a body of work. I have lots of skills. I studied art starting when I was seven or eight years old. My parents sent me to art school on weekends. I knew from an early age how to paint, how to draw, how to build things. I was surrounded by people who did that with great dexterity.

"But for me, the idea of making the perfect rendition or drawing of a flower or person has no challenge. Even the idea of photographing it has no interest. It seems to me that this is an end point rather than a launching off point, because the craft is defined by your capabilities of being able to render it appropriately. Assuming you have the skills to render that flower," says China Blue, "what else is left?" Realism, for her, is just not interesting.

For China Blue, the most important job an artist has is to challenge and expand the definition of art. "I want to take art beyond the technical. To be able to add on to art, to be able to extend what art is, that is my interest.

"The best artists, people like John Cage or Picasso, refused to accept what the past had told them was a successful approach to making art. They did something completely different. They extended the definition of what art is. That is what I am trying to do.

"Some say that I operate in the margins of the art world," she continues. "I see this as a compliment, because I do not want to be doing what everyone else is doing. I can paint. I can draw. I can make all kinds of different traditional shapes and forms. I can do it, but if everyone else is doing it, it seems silly to me to be stepping on common turf.

> John Cage (1912-1992) was an American composer who incorporated "found sound"—sound from the environment or noise—into his music. His best known work is his 1952 composition "4'33"—four minutes and 33 seconds of silence.

"When I think about art—about my ambitions for my art—I think about how I want to spend my time. My interest is in approaching subjects from a unique viewpoint. I want to find something primary in the topic. And sound—the sound of an object—the actual vibrations that are moving through the object—these are like the DNA of the acoustic world. This is exciting.

"Spending my time drawing the same tree over and over again does not sustain my interest. What I found more interesting is recording the tree, listening to what the tree has to say, and listening to how it responds to its environment, what is going on in the tree."

Extending Art

That China Blue seeks to extend the definition of art is clear in her work. Her latest exhibitions—*Catching Fireflies* and *Fireflies 2.0*—are what she defines as "artbots," art and robots merged. She describes the work as "informed by DIY [do it yourself] aesthetics." Her work combines the latest trends in home repair with art. In fact, one piece, entitled *Firefly 2.0*, was displayed in the hornet-killing section of a hardware store.

Firefly in a Jar

The sculpture features a small robot, shaped like a hornet, sitting inside a Ball wide-mouth mason jar. The robot's body contains a blue LED and flashes, just as a giant bug—a cross between a hornet and a firefly—might.

China Blue describes the work as being "made out of 'upcycled' materials"—recycled materials that have a new use. The "bugs," she explains, "skitter unpredictably while flashing a large blue LED." They

Firefly Bright Bot

are lit from within, so the light appears to be part of its "natural" body, like the light in a firefly. China Blue wants the work to suggest a "whimsical" time and to "harken back to wonderful summertime childhood experiences collecting bugs."

She explains further, "The artbot is based on BEAM robotic technology, using simple analog circuits." China Blue is, as she says, "inspired by the idea of the emergence of new living forms from the wastes of older ones." Waste today includes electronic components and power sources, old computers, cell phones, and electrical units that we just throw away.

Is there a potential for "new forms to arise" from this waste? Might these forms be "scavengers" that "build on the waste of their predecessors?" There is a kind of science fiction element in her work, and also a challenge to a 21st-century lifestyle that tosses away electronics as "waste." To see a video of her installation, go to www.chinablueart.com

China Blue explains that, for her, art "is a flexing condition. I am more motivated by ideas than by imagery. And because of that, my work changes often.

"*Fireflies* resulted from what I see as the beginning of an inquiry based on electronic investigations that I have been doing for the last couple of years." She has been studying electronics and building her own devices. She taught herself to solder and to make what she calls "circuit-driven constructions."

"While I have been doing this," she continues, "I am asking myself, 'Where is the art in this? Is there an opportunity to make art out of circuit-driven things? What would I do and how would this translate into art as opposed to another electronic doo-dad that is really seen as a toy?'"

For China Blue, the answer is the exhibition. She was able to take "small electronic things and incorporate them into sculptures to create interactive motion-driven works.

"There are plants with variegated leaves that are triggered to move based on the amount of light available; there are crickets chirping but they are electronic; they turn on when the light available is turned off. So there is a circuit attached to the crickets, and they function like normal crickets would in the natural world by chirping with low light. It is nice, since we cannot normally see crickets when they are chirping anyway, and in the exhibit, the crickets can be heard but not seen.

"There is a cast form based on a rhizome that is illuminated from the back by an LED. The LED is triggered by a probe that is attached to a vial of water. The plant has to be watered regularly, just as a natural plant does. When the vial dries out, the plant light turns off."

She explains, "The exhibit talks about the transition from a nature-driven society to a computer-based society, one that intersects with the natural world. It is an inquiry that is just beginning. I am not yet sure where it leads. But it is very much a comment on how technology has impacted society. The exhibit provides one idea of what our future, or how our future, might evolve. It suggests ways that technology is quickly changing our world."

She adds that this was her first effort at "working with technology in a really in-depth way" and incorporating that into her art. "Because I was building some of my own circuitry, I started to think about circuitry equipment and wiring as resources for making art. This experience also made me realize that this is a gender-based topic. I find that almost every male I have ever known is very comfortable with these aspects, but I had no exposure to any of this and had to develop a comfort level. As I did, I became more exposed to circuitry and realized how valuable it is. Slowly the ideas started to evolve.

"I learned also from failures. When working with circuitry and electronics, you have to assume and absorb a lot of failures. This is something that I am still waiting to adjust to. Failure is not something that I like and want to embrace, but I have to. You have to assume that the first, second, and third time you build a circuit, it will not work. If it works the very first time, then you are probably going to have problems down the road. This was a growth experience for me.

"I also added functionality to sculpture. So no longer is sculpture something that just sits on the shelf. Now it is active and interactive. Somehow, the sculpture creates a relationship to the world, in its physicality, in its motion, in its sonic engagement. It has a kind of presence."

Eiffel Tower

China Blue's recording of the Eiffel Tower resulted from her exploration of the Tower's presence in the world.

"I am fascinated by the idea of the Eiffel Tower and have been for many, many years," she says. "I am also interested in how sound shapes space." She is concerned not only with acoustics but on how buildings "talk," on how "people who live and work in a space" interact with it, make sounds and communicate with their environment, and "how that could be translated into art."

She explains that before she began the Eiffel Tower project, "I was creating sound-based installations that would recreate the acoustics that I could record in various environments. I found this fascinating. From the sculptural point of view, I saw sound as the material used to fill a space. Just as if you were casting something, you would be dealing with the actual physical materi-

al that fills a void. This is the metaphor that I was working with. So I did a number of large-scale installations around the world—Dijon, Finland, New York—where I made pieces that recreated building acoustics. And this brought me to the Eiffel Tower."

She became the first person to record the Eiffel Tower. "It was interesting to me, because the Eiffel Tower is a kind of icon that represents a place that people find fascinating, that they are attracted to for so many reasons. I was interested in capturing that fascination. I had no expectations of what I would be recording, and that was probably quite good, because what I ended up with was beyond anything I could have imagined."

She recorded from two different viewpoints: first, "the ambient acoustic viewpoint, all the different levels including the ground level," and second, "the actual vibrations of the structure."

"The idea, recording the vibrations of the structure for their acoustic richness, is not common," she explains. "Normally, people record the vibrations of the structure to identify the flaws in the building. It is a construction application and not an artistic application. But I wanted something more than what is usual.

"Fortunately," she laughs, "since I was doing this in France, and since French people love absurd approaches to art, the idea was embraced."

China Blue and her team were allowed to "crawl around with microphones. The result was fantastic. We got sounds that I could never have hoped to manufacture and the result was acoustically spectacular." For more about this project, see http://www.chinablueart.com/EiffelTower.htm.

Education: Visual Arts—2D to 3D

China Blue's education is as a visual artist. "I went to the California College of the Arts in Oakland, California, and then I got my masters at Hunter College in New York City. I got my bachelor and masters degrees later than is typical, not in the normal evolution of going to college right after high school. I took a break and did a lot of other things."

She struggled with her love of art. "My father and mother are both artists. My father is a ceramist and my mother made jewelry. My father told me that I should never think of art as a career choice. I should think of it as a hobby. When I was growing up, there was no career in art. There were no opportunities to sell art.

"In addition, I think my father believes that you should make art for yourself and not for your audience. He said that if you make art and show it in a gallery, you are going to have to compromise what you make for marketing purposes. And I have indeed discovered that this is absolutely true."

But China Blue realized that art was the only thing that she wanted to do with her life. "I decided that I was wasting a lot of time doing things that I had no commitment to, that were just dull and boring, that I was rolling from job to job. I realized that I needed to focus on what I wanted to do with my life. I needed to take a risk, and study art."

She adds, "It is not in my personality trait to take on big risks. I hate risks."

Interestingly, she does not see her decision to record the Eiffel Tower, to climb all over the Tower with a microphone, as a risk. "That was just an inquiry," she says, and laughs.

When she began studying at California College of the Arts, China Blue planned to establish a career as a painter, but she quickly discovered, as she explains, that her "interest was not in two-dimensional space but in three-dimensional space, and so my plan changed quite dramatically. I started making paintings, and they became physical objects. They came off the wall, walked into the room and across the floor. I was not painting imagery, I was building it."

Redefining Success

"When I decided to study art in college," China Blue continues, "I realized that I needed to redefine success, for myself." It is not about making money or being famous. "In art," she says, "there is success in being able to make a good piece, something that satisfies you. Success comes from not being afraid to delve into new terrain or learn new techniques. The work that I have done in the last fifteen years is based on techniques that I developed myself, and I would never have done that if I did not find that following my own interests is essential. Success comes by my not being afraid to follow my own interests and inspirations, especially when they are in far left field. I have found that this is when those interests bring me to a place that is really fascinating."

Another essential for success, says China Blue, is a sustaining and supportive environment, friends and colleagues who help each other and whose opinions, ideas, and critiques she trusts. "It is important to have an environment of friends to sustain you," she says, "and to keep you on track.

"Being an artist in the United States can be hard," she adds. "It is seen as really an odd thing to be doing. As an artist, you experience that nearly every day. People think it is weird. Why would you bother? When you leave the United States, it is a completely different thing, especially in Europe. There, people see artists almost as gods and goddesses, as people doing something beyond anything that they could ever have done, as something super, super, super special. In the United States, I find that I have to say, hesitantly, 'Well, I am an artist.' When people in Europe ask, I say it with confidence, and they go ballistic and say that is so phenomenal."

To date, China Blue has found her greatest success with her work on recording the Vertical Gun at NASA. She explains, "The gun is three stories high and shoots vertically downwards into a chamber to mimic the impact of asteroids and meteors, especially on the moon's surface. My proposal was, 'Have you guys thought about the sounds that are associated with this research?'

"These scientists," she continues, "had never thought of that. They were saying, 'What are you talking about?' But since my project, now they think about the sounds associated with the gun and are excited about that. I changed the way they think about their work. That is something I am really proud of.

"I have found, as an artist, that you have to follow your own interests. Don't be scared of trying new techniques, if these are needed to take your work to new dimensions. Don't be afraid to put the pieces together and to find new pieces.

"Art is not about technical training—about drawing that tree—it is about inquiry, figuring out how the world works. Do not be afraid to ask the big questions. And, most important, do not be afraid to go where the answers lead."

CHAPTER 9

Henry Diltz

Photo used with permission.

Shooting the World

Henry Diltz is considered by many to be "the" rock and roll photographer. For nearly fifty years, his work has graced hundreds of album covers and has been featured in books, magazines, and newspapers. He has produced powerful photographic essays of Woodstock, The Monterey Pop Festival, The Doors, Crosby, Stills, Nash & Young, Jimi Hendrix, and others. He shot more than 200 album covers—including the first albums of Jackson Browne, The Eagles, and Crosby, Stills & Nash.

A founding member of the Modern Folk Quartet, Diltz entered photography through music. The pictures began with a $20 second-hand Japanese camera purchased while he was on tour. When Modern Folk Quartet disbanded, he began his photographic career almost by accident, with an album cover for The Lovin' Spoonful.

More than 500 of Diltz's photos, taken between 1966 and 1975, have been collected and published in California Dreaming *(Genesis Publications, 2008). He is a partner in, and is exclusively published and represented by, the Morrison Hotel Gallery.*

In this chapter, Diltz discusses the relationship between music and visual arts—the ways he captures musicians on film—and the importance of being open to new opportunities.

Scroll through Henry Diltz's photographic credits and you will see that he has had almost unlimited access to artists as diverse as Jackson Browne, Paul McCartney, Joni Mitchell, David Cassidy, Tom Waits, The Eagles, America, Richard Pryor, Keith Richards, Neil Young, The Monkees, Linda Ronstadt, and Truman Capote. Yet, nearly fifty years after he began with the Modern Folk Quartet (MFQ), he remains humble, down-to-earth, and very much like the musician he was then, doing, as he describes, "concerts at college campuses and clubs."

Diltz considers it almost an act of fate, that, while traveling with MFQ, he stopped at a small store in East Lansing, Michigan, bought a second-hand camera, and started taking snapshots. As he remembers, when they returned home, "We had a slide show with our friends. Seeing all these recent moments huge and glowing on the wall hooked me immediately. From that moment onwards, I was a photographer."

> Modern Folk Quartet was an American folk group formed in 1962 by Henry Diltz, Cyrus Faryar, Chip Douglas, and Stan White.

Diltz takes very little credit for his success. "Somewhere in the 1960s I read a book called *Autobiography of a Yogi*[1], and it opened up another side of my life. In the 1960s, we were very concerned with trying to find out what life *really* was, what was it about. Jerry Garcia famously said after he first took LSD, 'I knew there was more going on than they were telling us.' In that spirit, in the 1960s, we did dabble in some of god's psychedelic things, god's herb, and it had a great deal to do with opening up one's viewpoint.

Jerry Garcia (1942-1995) was a founder of the American rock band The Grateful Dead, one of the key bands to represent the counterculture movement.

Crosby, Stills & Nash is a folk rock group comprised of David Crosby (1941-), Stephen Stills (1945-), and Graham Nash (1942-).

"I'm a big student of letting the universe decide," he explains. "Just be open to what opportunities come along. We have free will and we can go or not go with every impulse that comes along, and it is surprising where it leads when you look back at it later.

"I don't know why I was in the place that I was when I was with the camera in my hand. But it has resulted in a very successful career and the creation of a visual history of rock and roll."

Diltz continues, "People have said, 'Thank you for being there and capturing all that.' But I don't take credit in an egotistical way. I think: 'Look, I was just there. I saw it and I photographed it. I didn't make that picture. I saw it, and it happened, and I clicked.'

"But then I think: Well, I guess I was the guy who got it all down.' If I wasn't there, somebody would have taken the *Crosby, Stills & Nash* album cover. It wouldn't have been the same, but *someone* would have taken it. I think of all the pictures that I took. Some of them have become well known, kind of iconic, and I think I feel lucky to have been there at that time and place, ready to do whatever the universe thrust upon me."

Crosby, Stills, and Nash

Education

Diltz summarizes his life this way: "Generally, I say, I was a folk musician, a photographer, who began photographing all my friends and that segued into a career in photography."

He was born in Kansas City in 1938, to parents who worked for Trans World Airlines (TWA). His father was a pilot, and his mother a flight attendant. They traveled a lot but landed in Great Neck, New York, where Diltz lived from kindergarten to third grade. Then, his father, who had joined the Army Air Corps, was killed in World War II. His mother remarried, and Diltz's stepfather was in the State Department.

"That began a life of real travel," says Diltz. "In 1947, we went to Tokyo. We were some of the first American civilians to live in Tokyo after the war. We lived in Tokyo for five years, and that had a great deal to do with my upbringing. Then I went from there to a small town in Michigan for the eighth grade. And then we were back in Bangkok, Thailand, which was another jolt, another way of looking at life."

From there, Diltz's family returned to Great Neck, where he graduated high school. He was about to begin studies at the University of Montana to major in wildlife management. "I was going to be a forest ranger," he recalls.

"But that summer, my Mom said, 'Your stepfather has been assigned to Bonn, Germany. Go to Montana, if you would like, or come with us to Germany.' And I was so excited about Montana. I had my dorm room and everything. I love the outdoors and animals. But I thought, 'Hmm, this is a good chance to go and see Europe. I can always go back to Montana.' That was the road not taken. I find in life you have those crossroads, those forks in the road, where you take the other choice."

Diltz went to Germany and believes that this experience enriched him. "Germany opened my life a tremendous amount, especially to classical music." He studied in Munich, at an overseas branch of the University of Maryland, "with all military kids, about 200 guys and girls," he explains. He spent two years there, focusing on psychology and classical music. He sang in the choir and traveled around the country.

From there Diltz faced another fork in the road. As the son of a deceased military person, he was eligible to take the exam to enter West Point. Many of his friends were planning to take the exam, so, "as a lark," says Diltz, "I took the exam and was accepted to West Point."

At first, Diltz "couldn't have cared less. I was going to hitchhike with a friend to Scandinavia that summer. But all the people at the college told me that this was a rare opportunity, and I thought, 'Oh my gosh. I guess I need to try this.'"

Diltz made another big change, took another road, and enrolled in West Point. His experience there was "fantastic. I am so glad that I went," he states. "And," he adds, "I am so glad that I left. That year was huge in my learning about life. I had been around the military my whole life and I loved it. I loved the long gray line. To this day, when I walk across a parking lot, I hum John Philip Sousa marches."

West Point and Folk Music

Pete Seeger (1919-), an American folk singer and 5-string banjo player, is one of the leaders of the 1950s and 1960s folk music revival.

Bob Gibson (1931-96) was a folk singer, banjo player, and guitarist, who helped lead the folk music revival in the 1950s and 1960s.

The Everly Brothers—Don (1937-) and Phil (1939-) —are a folk, country, and rock and roll duo that had fifteen Top 10 hits.

The Kingston Trio is an American folk music group that helped launch the folk revival in the late-1950s and early 1960s.

"But while I was at West Point, I joined the Columbia Record Club and started hearing folk music — Pete Seeger, Peggy Seeger, and Bob Gibson. I heard on the radio songs like 'Tom Dooley' by the Kingston Trio and 'Bye Bye Love' by The Everly Brothers."

Diltz was fascinated by banjo and folk music. After his first year at West Point, he decided not to return. Instead, he recalls, "I went as far away as I could go and still be in the U.S. school system." He went to the University of Hawaii, bought a banjo, and continued his studies in psychology.

He also "got totally into singing in a coffee house. Every night I would go to the Green Sleeves Coffee House in Honolulu. I formed groups with people and started singing in different clubs. Eventually, my friends and I formed a quartet and we called it the Lexington 4. Then we changed our name to the Modern Folk Quartet. This was in 1961. We decided to come to L.A. to seek our fortunes."

The Modern Folk Quartet, Diltz explains, "sang four-part harmony, which was different than most. Most folk groups have a three-part or two-part harmony. A three-part is just a triad, but when you have four parts, then, when you have a four-part chord, a zinger, like a 6th or a 9th, you can really give the music some body.

"We played a little club our first night in L.A., and we just wowed the place. We got a record company contract, a manager, and an agent right away. We traveled around and recorded for Warner Bros. Then we recorded some singles with Phil Spector, who was a big producer at the time and we traveled all over the country."

Phil Spector (1939-) is an American music producer who pioneered the "Wall of Sound," generating more than twenty-five Top 40 hits.

Diltz recalls, "In the early 1960s, folk music was huge. We would headline at colleges. It was during the Vietnam War, and of course any songs that were anti-war—'Draft Dodgers Rag' and 'I Ain't A-Marching Anymore' by Phil Ochs—were big. Dylan was starting to write music."

Folk music underwent a change at that time, explains Diltz. Before the 1960s, "We would sing actual folk songs—written by 'folks,' people like

Phil Ochs (1940-1976) was an American folk singer, songwriter, and activist whose songs reflected both his politics and sense of humor.

miners, sailors, cowboys, and pioneers—songs passed down from generation to generation. Then in the early 1960s, people started writing their own music. I try to trace it back. I think it was one of those ideas that everyone sort of got at the same time.

"Woody Guthrie wrote songs early on. He was one of the few guys who wrote songs, and Bob Dylan idolized Woody Guthrie. Dylan started writing songs. And you have James Taylor and Paul Simon and, a little later, Joni Mitchell and Jackson Browne. You had this whole generation of singer-songwriters. That was a whole new deal. They were still playing acoustic instruments, but now they were singing their own songs.

Woody Guthrie (1912-1967) was a songwriter and musician considered by many to be the father of American folk music.

James Taylor (1948-) is an American singer, songwriter, and guitarist, whose hits include "Fire and Rain" and "You've Got a Friend."

Paul Simon (1941-) is a 12-time Grammy-winning singer-songwriter, whose hits include "Kodachrome" and "Loves Me Like a Rock."

Joni Mitchell (1943-), born Roberta Joan Anderson, is a Canadian musician and one of the greatest songwriters of the 20th century.

"Then the Beatles played Ed Sullivan in 1964. That was a huge turning point for folk music. Everyone saw the Beatles play, and we all traded in our stand-up basses for electric, and we electrified our guitars." The Modern Folk Quartet went electric as well.

Jackson Browne (1948-) is an American folk and rock singer-songwriter, whose biggest hits include "Doctor My Eyes" and "Running on Empty."

Recalls Diltz, "We started playing psychedelic folk rock and we were getting popular."

An Accidental Photographer

This popularity increased tours and one of these tours led to Michigan and that little store with second-hand cameras. Diltz recalls, "On one of our tours across the country, doing colleges and clubs, we were in a camper and we stopped in Michigan at a store with a table full of second-hand cameras. One of the guys in the group said, 'Cameras, oh, I'll have one of those.' And I said, 'Well, I will get one, too.'

The Beatles, comprised of John Lennon (1940-1980), Paul McCartney (1942-), George Harrison (1943-2001), and Ringo Starr (1940-), is the most influential band in the history of popular music. From 1964 to 1970, they earned 20 number one singles and 14 number one albums.

The Ed Sullivan Show (1948-1971), formerly Talk of the Town, was a popular and influential variety television show that aired on Sunday nights.

"I had never thought of it before, and it became a fun thing to do in our motor home. One of the guys said, 'Pull into the next drug store,' and he went in to buy film. And I said, 'How do you load this?' and 'What are these numbers?'

"We spent the next few weeks photographing everything we did and each other. When we got back to L.A., we developed the film and, lo and behold, it was slide film. I did not know the difference and I said, 'Well, look at this. Let's get a projector and have a slide show.'

"My first huge epiphany was that slide show," says Diltz. It was mind-blowing that you could see all these moments recreated huge and on the wall. And I thought, 'My God, we have to take more of these.' I was so excited to take more pictures, so we could have another slide show the next weekend.

"I started photographing my friends," says Diltz, "my close friends, and some were Stephen Stills, Mama Cass, David Crosby. These were all friends of mine in the music business."

Diltz says that his second epiphany came when he realized that he could earn money from his photographs. He went to a sound check with Buffalo Springfield—a folk group that included Neil Young, Stephen Stills, Richie Furay, and Jim Messina. "While they were in the club," says Diltz, "I was walking around taking photos for my slide show. I saw a big mural outside just as the guys walked out and I asked them, 'Hey, you guys. Stand right there in front of that mural, so I can show what size it is.' I did not think of this as a group shot.

Cass Elliott (1941-74), born Ellen Naomi Cohen—also known as Mama Cass—was an American singer who was a member of the folk group The Mamas and the Papas.

Buffalo Springfield

"But a week later, I got a call from a teenybopper magazine and they said, 'We hear you have a picture of Buffalo Springfield. We would love to run that, and we will pay you $100.' And—boing! That was the second epiphany, that somebody would actually pay me for doing this thing that I was spending all my time and musician money on—film and processing. This could actually earn money.

"From then on," says Diltz, "I was off and running."

Album Covers

The Doors was an American rock band led by charismatic singer Jim Morrison (1943-71), who died of an overdose at 27.

America is a folk rock band whose biggest hits are "A Horse with No Name," "Tin Man," "Lonely People," and "Sister Golden Hair."

Jimmy Webb (1946-) is a Grammy-winning composer whose songs include "Up, Up, and Away," "Wichita Lineman," and "McArthur Park."

"All of my pictures," says Diltz, "started getting used for album covers and one thing and another. Along the way, I teamed up with a graphic artist, and we started doing album covers for Crosby, Stills & Nash, The Eagles, The Doors, Joni Mitchell, America, and Jimmy Webb. We did maybe 100 album covers."

"The album cover itself was an amazing art form," Diltz says. "It was a 12-inch square, and this was before MTV and VH1. People got their idea of the group by holding the cover. There was something about it. You would put the album on and then sit back and look at the picture or read all the liner notes. I did it myself. Everybody did it. People are constantly telling me, 'I don't know how many hours I stared at that picture.'

"This is something that has passed," says Diltz. "There are no longer albums and so, no covers. With the little CD, even if there is a booklet, you don't sit and stare at it, so that is a change. And even CDs are a thing of the past, in a way. Now the change is digital."

But Diltz does not lament the end of the album cover. He sees today's world as connected in new ways. "You can email songs," he says. "We have become so connected. We twitter and tweet. It is a whole new thing and it is great. We are connected in a way as human beings."

Connections

It is this kind of connection that Diltz tries to create with his photography.

Says Diltz, "I went on the road with so many musicians and saw the world, all around the world. I did a world tour first with David Cassidy. Then later years, Garth Brooks was a guy that I photographed a lot and traveled around with. So although, I had already seen the world as a young kid, I got to see it again as an adult.

David Cassidy (1950-) is an American singer and actor best known for his role as Keith on the 1970s sitcom *The Partridge Family*.

Garth Brooks (1962-) is an American country singer and musician who has sold more than 130 million albums.

"I have a great affinity with people from around the world. I find that I understand and have a feeling about people. You know, I studied psychology because I was fascinated by people, what made them quirky. So here was a way of putting all that together — the music, the psychology. I call photography a passport into people's lives — where you would not ordinarily be."

Diltz takes photos in the documentary style, "fly on the wall, I call it," he says. "I don't use lights and a big studio. I go to where the people are and shoot."

A career high point came for Diltz when he was asked to photograph Truman Capote. "One day, my phone rang and it was someone from *Rolling Stone* magazine. They asked, 'What are you doing this afternoon?' And I said, 'Well, nothing really.' And they said, 'Can you get on a plane, fly to Palm Springs, and photograph Truman Capote? We need a cover for *Rolling Stone*. We have the whole story but no cover photo.'"

Continues Diltz, "I had studied Truman Capote in Munich at the University of Maryland. He was like this

Truman Capote (1924-1984) was an American author whose best known works are *Breakfast at Tiffany's* (1958) and *In Cold Blood* (1966).

huge figure to me. And I just knocked on the door in Palm Springs, and, my God, there was Truman Capote. And he said, 'Come on in.' We spent an hour talking and taking photos and that was a cover of *Rolling Stone*. And I thought, 'Thank you, God.'"

Framing

For Diltz, photography is all about framing. "I always wanted what I saw in real life to look like the picture. This is the way you frame it: What you crop out and what you focus on, what your eye sees and what you think is interesting and important. I guess that depends on the person, and I guess I was lucky that all my friends were interested in what I saw. I would try to make it interesting by finding moments of colorful or funny things. In a sense, it was a holdover from being in show business, from being a musician. That was about entertaining people and this was a way of entertaining people.

"For me," says Diltz, "photography is my take on life, what I consider important. That includes people, all the people that I see. Many times, I am hired to shoot a person, to photograph somebody that I never met before. So how do I do that? I meet the person and bond with them. And in the back of my mind, I am figuring out how they look to me. So that I get the essence of them and I try to get that in my picture somehow by capturing a moment or an angle, and that is the fine part of it.

"I used to worry a lot about it. I used to think, 'Oh, my God. I am going to take photos of someone. What if I can't do it, can't figure them out? What if it doesn't work out?' But now I just look forward to it and think that whatever happens will be perfect.

Diltz encourages artists to continue to study their craft. "I am a great student. When digital came into being, I swore I would never shoot digital. 'I am a film guy,' I said. But now I shoot totally digital. This is just a revolution in photography, nothing to be afraid of. And it has made many things easier.

"In the old days, if you shot photos, you would spend a good part of a week getting proof sheets made and getting film developed. Now, you come home, you download, you email the photos, or you FedEx the disc. It is so immediate. And I have the pictures and they have the pictures. I can send the photos to the manager, the record company, the group. And I can keep them. I mean, everyone has them.

"So now, my life is all about scanning the stuff that I did back in the 1960s and 1970s, because I get calls every day from books, magazines, video companies, and even museums. They want to use this stuff. That is a wonderful thing."

For Diltz, his photography and his art is all about communication. As he puts it, "Art is how we communicate to one another and to the world. It is how we express our existence, our aliveness, like a rooster crows or a whale sings. They are saying, 'I am here. I am alive.'

"We are lucky to have more varied forms of expression, more sophisticated means of expressions. We have more notes to work with and hands that can play many instruments. We have eight notes to arrange in infinite ways and many instruments to play them. We have paints of many colors and hands and feet to color and dance, to say, 'Here, here I am. This is how I feel about being me. This is how I feel about being alive.' I guess that is what I do with my pictures. I am saying: 'I am here.' I didn't really intend to be a rock and roll historian, but that is what I have done with my pictures. I have documented rock music."

Jane Goodall (1934-) is a British anthropologist and primatologist, who is considered to be the world's leading expert on chimpanzees.

Says Diltz, "I am an observer. I love to interact with people, but I love to *watch* them. I think of myself as the Jane Goodall of rock photography. I am sure she would hate to hear that," he laughs, "but I mean that I don't want to disturb my subject. Just as she would sit there with her pad and paper and not want to disturb the chimps but instead watch and record them, that is what I like to do. I like to watch people and take candid photos of them whenever possible. That is when you can really catch something about a person."

"When you get older," says Diltz, "it is easy to look back and think, 'Boy, if that hadn't happened, then I wouldn't have done this,' but when you are in the middle of it, it is a little harder to reflect. You don't know what is going to happen. So I say to people starting out today, 'Try to be passionate—be passionate about the things you love. And relax. Have a little faith that things are going to work out. Just go through life with your camera and let it happen. Let it unfold.'"

Note

1. Yogananda, Paramhansa. *Autobiography of a Yogi*, LA: Self-realization Fellowship, 1946. Print.

CHAPTER 10

Lori Landay

Photo used with permission.

Visual Meaning—Technology, Art, and Culture

Lori Landay is Associate Professor of Cultural Studies at Berklee College of Music in Boston. She is also a new media artist and interdisciplinary scholar exploring the making of visual meaning in twentieth- and twenty first-century American culture.

Landay earned a Bachelor of Arts from Colby College, a Master of Arts in English from Indiana University, a second Master of Arts from Boston College in American Studies, and a Ph.D. in English and American Studies from Indiana University.

She is the author of two books: I Love Lucy *(2010) and* Madcaps, Screwballs, and Con Women: The Female Trickster in American Culture *(1998). She has also published journal articles, book chapters, and multimedia online journal pieces on other aspects of film and television comedy, silent film, and new media technologies. She is the writer, director, and editor of the documentary film* The Jazz Age Gaze: Looking at the Flapper Film, *and numerous "machinima" digital videos, as well as the creator of virtual art installations and other digital art. She is also L1Aura Loire in the virtual world Second Life, and L1Loire in OpenSim and other virtual world platforms.*

Landay has earned numerous awards including a National Endowment for the Humanities Enduring Questions Grant and a Newbury Comics Faculty Fellowship.

In this chapter, Landay discusses the ways that new technologies foster art in the twenty first century.

In her art, her scholarship, and her teaching, Lori Landay—a professor, writer, visual artist, and cultural studies expert—knows how important it is to examine a subject through multiple lenses. Such an interdisciplinary examination increases understanding and benefits the thinker and the artist. For Landay, this examination always includes technology. She is interested in that moment when technology loses its strangeness and becomes "natural."

> Both OpenSim (OpenSimulator) and Second Life are computer applications that enable people to create virtual worlds via the internet.

Landay has been interested in computers and computer programming since she was a child in the 1970s "when there were still punch cards," she laughs. "I started doing word processing back when it was all text and line editing, and I watched this real shift to the graphical user interface, to the point and click and all of that." She finds fascinating the way that technology has "democratized what people can do."

Another important concern for her involves connecting what she describes as her "creative side" with her "scholarly" or "critical side."

"For me," she says, "that has always been the biggest challenge. I feel like in my recent work, I have found a medium—virtual art—with the plasticity, the malleability that allows me to move back and forth between those two aspects."

Landay's art and scholarship are not separate. "I don't really see the creative and the critical as different. Being able to think through the ideas as I work on a creative expression of them, and then being able to move back into a critical explanation of them—in my mind, there is not really a big division there. And once we start using virtual art and new media, those lines break down even more easily."

Storyteller

Landay considers herself, primarily, a storyteller. "I tell stories in a lot of different ways," she explains. "I am very interested in narrative. Even in the least narrative pieces that I make, there are stories and experiences to be had, to be created and shaped."

She recalls, as a child, "making books and illustrating them, making plays and getting kids in my neighborhood to make plays. That part of it—putting on plays, telling stories, writing stories and illustrating them—that I have carried with me throughout my life."

Even when Landay went to graduate school to study literature and culture, she never left behind the creative side. "I was supposed to be writing research papers, but I kept wanting to illustrate them. Or I would become really interested in choosing the film frames that I would discuss in a paper. I would put four frames together, and as I started to work on that, people would say, is this a paper or a comic book?

"At that time, I started making music videos for my friends who were in bands. When there was this turn to people having laptops and their own video cameras, I learned editing. As soon as filmmaking became digitized, I started to do that as well. When I was putting together the manuscript for my first book—*Madcaps, Screwballs, and Con Women*—I had so many illustrations that the editor refused to take them all. I realized that the pictures and images were just as important to me as the words.

"In graduate school, one of my professors told me that I might be too creative to have a traditional academic career. At first, I did not know what that meant. But I have thought about this at different times in my life, as I was developing my career, and I thought about what work makes me happiest, what choices give me the widest range to explore this idea about the division between critical and creative work.

"I came to realize that this is an artificial division, and people get trained one way or another. But the two parts are really helpful together. It is important for students, especially students who are working in the arts, to see that theory and production are not separate. They need to be good at both critical and creative thinking. Even if artists do not have a theoretical background, don't have that vocabulary, they are still working with those concepts. This is why art students take 'studies' classes—literary studies, music history, art history."

Landay carries her commitment to join theory and production into her teaching. "I do this as more of an experiential undertaking than any kind of 'professional' way. If I am teaching a film history class, I will ask students to make something in the spirit of silent film, for instance. For me, unifying theory and practice has been a good thing as an artist, and it has enriched my scholarship."

"My goals," says Landay, simply, "are to express myself and to help others see the things I think are most important. Artists see things that are familiar in ways that are different, or they see new things and want to share that vision or perception with others. It is not enough just to see it yourself. You want to show that to others. You want to represent that concept and share that with someone else."

Most recently, Landay has begun exploring the world through virtual art and media. "One of the things that I am most excited about right now," she explains, "is *machinima*—a neologism, a word put together: machine and cinema. It means capturing what is on the screen when you are in the virtual world or are in another 3-D or video game environment." (See her numerous "machinima" digital videos available on vimeo.com and YouTube.)

Landay, a film critic and expert, makes movies, but instead of "finding a physical location and trying to find actors, and using a real camera, I use my computer screen as the camera and film in the virtual world. I have a couple of avatars, and I set up scenes as if those avatars were actors. The computer and the virtual world become a movie-making tool kit. It is a very interesting kind of digital filmmaking. I am not really an animator, because I am not creating all the objects, although I am putting them together. The movies I make are composed of a real mash-up of things that are found in the virtual world, things that other people have created. I get permission to film them. I create some things. I write a screenplay, a script, and I make a film."

A recent work is in the silent film style with inter-titles. "Other pieces that I have done," she explains, "are really more educational." She describes a video where she is speaking to her avatar: "The real me and my avatar discuss concepts about the virtual world," she says.

Integrating Technology into Our Lives

For Landay, being able to move between actual footage and virtual footage enables her to explore one of the ideas about technology that excites her the most: "How do we integrate technology into our lives, especially the technology that has become so much a part of our everyday that we don't even think about it anymore? How do we move back and forth quickly between using and not using technology?"

Landay references the telephone. "In the beginning, it was a big deal to make a phone call. You would talk to an operator who physically, with a wire, patched you through to another person. Now it all seems seamless, automatic, almost magical. We accept the seamlessness. It does not make us feel strange or alienated.

"Today," she continues, "most of us don't even think about the technology behind sending someone an email or a text anymore. You think about the message. But at the beginning, when you first started using that technology, you would think, 'Oh, what is that? What is that intrusion?' Then you got used to it, and it just became part of everyday life."

She continues, "When there is a new kind of technology, we feel that strangeness. I am interested in that place where there is that new technology, where it feels strange, just before we come to accept it and are transformed by it."

Landay believes that "everyone develops his or her own relationship to technology. For me, it has been very interesting to embrace new technology and explore what it can do. Some of the pieces that I have made are about testing technology, putting some new technology or a new technique through its paces and seeing if I can make something with that. Some products are more successful than others. I would encourage any artist of any medium to see what new tools and techniques, whether they are technological or not, are available. This is an interesting way to branch out and work.

"For my art," she continues, "I try to find what is new. I can set up installations that have sound, that can have a simulation of being as big as a building or a whole planet, where you, as your avatar, can be very small, as big as a real person, or huge. I can build a soundscape and you can move through it. The sound can change as you walk. I can set up things, so that when your avatar clicks on something with your mouse, suddenly you are transformed into doing an animation. I can change the camera position, so you are seeing what I want you to see. I can play video around you. I can play different kinds of music or sound. It is more than creating an installation. It is creating an immersive, interactive, sensory experience. As the technology gets better, the feeling of immersion will also improve."

Creative Documentary

Bridging the critical and the creative has led Landay to a new art form, the creative documentary. "These are like weird documentaries," she laughs. "We tend to think of documentaries as real and factual. Creative documentaries tend to say, 'Okay, a documentary is not fiction, it is not a story, but it is not necessarily that kind of voice of god with a narrator telling you exactly how things are.' A creative documentary can explore a concept in a way that is personal or funny. It may blend genres, move into animations, take the idea of nonfiction filmmaking and push the boundaries in various ways."

Landay has recently made a creative documentary about flapper films, entitled *The Jazz Age Gaze: Looking at the Flapper Film.* She describes her flapper film as "a compilation that also tries to present a visual argument." She uses images of flappers, of women from 1920s advertising to explore the connection between film and images of flappers in the 1920s cosmetics industry.

Says Landay, "Makeup is a commodity that was not always a part of everyday life for everyday women. Then, very

"Flapper" is a term for women of the 1920s who wore short skirts, applied excessive makeup, bobbed their hair, openly drank, and smoked.

quickly, by the mid-1920s, makeup became commonplace. That is interesting to me. How did the technology of cosmetics happen? How does makeup become a part of style, and what has the impact been on women, on society?

"Film has a lot to do with that normalizing of makeup—with defining style, manners, and women's comportment. So, in my film, I made an argument about that but not in a documentary kind of way, but instead, in a 'Here are lots of images and draw your own conclusions' kind of way. The viewer sees the associations that I make visually and through story."

A New Audience

With the new technology comes a new audience. Landay is not making art to be viewed in a gallery, nor is she making films to be seen in a theater, although her machinima films have been screened in those types of places. She is producing videos for an audience that is, "amorphous, the audience of the global internet." For Landay, this is another fascinating aspect of new media.

"I put my machinima videos on YouTube and they get hundreds and hundreds of hits. People sometimes leave comments. I have no idea who is watching them. People may even show a piece at a conference or some other event and then, all of a sudden, there will be a spike in viewers. There is one machinima I made called, 'What Is Second Life?' to explain what Second Life is. I made it primarily for my students, but it has been really helpful for a lot of people. People have seen this and asked me to make other pieces."

Some of Landay's work, under her avatar L1Aura Loire, exists in virtual art galleries and virtual museums, including the Fiteiro Cultural Center in Second Life. Each of her pieces has an elaborate story and helps emphasize the ideas that she finds most important—storytelling, communication, and integration of technology. Machinima is a way of showing what is in a virtual world or game to people who haven't experienced it themselves, as well as a tool for making animated movies that can stand alone.

One of her favorite pieces, that shows the way that she works and her artistic process, is called "Peony Envy."

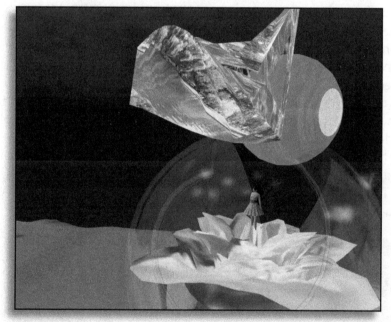

Peony envy

"Bloomington, Indiana, where I went to graduate school, is a real garden city. People have these amazing peony bushes. I was walking around one day and I thought, 'Everyone's peonies are so much better than mine. I have peony envy.' That is a real thing in a place that has the kind of competitive gardening that can be found in the Midwest. It was only when I was in the virtual world that I could create a sculpture that could express visually and imaginatively that concept of peony envy."

For Landay, the virtual world is a place where art can make metaphors come to life.

"I make these sculptures that start as animations," she explains. "One is based on the poem 'Desert Places' by Robert Frost, which is about snow. You go into the sphere and you get a notecard with the poem on it. You read the poem. The whole experience in that sphere is about the poem. So there is a snowscape and there is the howling wind sound, and it looks like snow and is all made out of ice.

"I like art that includes sound and text and moving images and visuals, real life action as well as graphics. I like to mix everything together."

One of her favorite virtual art pieces is based on the poem "Opal" by Amy Lowell. "You are ice and fire,/The touch of you burns my hands like snow."

Robert Frost (1874-1963) was a four-time Pulitzer-winning poet, best known for writing about New England, nature, and aspects of everyday life.

"This poem," says Landay, "has lots of contrast. I created two spheres, one for freezing and one for melting. You click, and your avatar does the animation, staying in a pose to become part of the sculpture. There are icicles that are melting and icicles break off, cracking, different kinds of sounds, and then there is ice fire, flaming up, and so this is the idea of taking an experience and a soundscape and joining a short poem with that."

Amy Lowell (1874-1925) was an American poet of the Imagist movement, who posthumously won the Pulitzer Prize in 1926 for *What's O'Clock*.

Landay is attracted to virtual media, because it allows her to make something quickly and to push boundaries. For instance, she explains, "I made a screwball comedy. I filmed avatars on sets and in already-existing locations in the virtual world, included my sculpture 'Peony Envy' as a prop for a character to hide in, but I couldn't decide what the best ending would be. Then, instead of just one ending, I came up with a multitude of endings, because I couldn't decide.

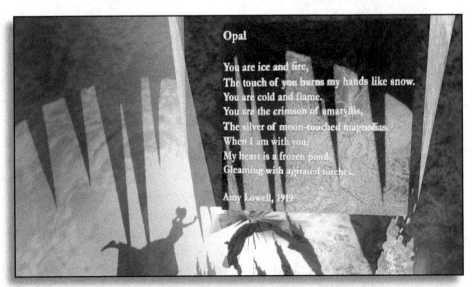

Opal

"The screwball comedies from the 1930s all end with a marriage or the promise of a marriage or a remarriage. That is the 1930s ending. What is the twenty-first century ending? I made it more postmodern with a variety of endings.

"In one ending, all three characters fall from the sky and land in different places. In another ending, the characters drop from the sky again, but now, they are in a black and white film noir scene, and the main characters are still in color. I like being able to experiment to see what can happen. I like to mix techniques.

"Anything that is digital can be reworked endlessly. It is very malleable. It fosters a kind of reluctance to finish because there is always a new technique possible. I titled that film 'Open End: A Digital Silent Film Screwball Comedy about Irresolution' to call attention to and make fun of that."

How Culture Works

As she plays with technology, Landay also explores culture.

Through her art and her scholarship, she seeks to increase people's awareness of how culture works. As she explains, "Some of my pieces—the immersive pieces where you click on something and you see something different, because your camera perspective has been taken—change your point of view. I want people to become more conscious of how we experience the world through our own point of view, and to consider the ways that different points of view are forced upon us.

"What is the point of view that you have been forced to accept? How can we keep our own point of view? How can we retain our individuality *and* be part of the crowd? How we can share experiences with other people and have our own unique perspective?"

In an installation in a virtual world, or in a film like 'Open End' that plays with the idea of different possible outcomes and genres, Landay constructs a reality. From this, she hopes that people see that reality, culture, is constructed. "The more people are aware that culture is constructed, and how it is constructed, the more savvy a participant in culture and society they can be. The more they understand that things aren't the way they are, because that is the way they have to be, but that they were constructed to be that way, the more we can understand and interact with our world. That makes them better citizens, better neighbors, better members of a community.

"They can also understand that the world used to be different and can and will be different in the future. It opens people up to the idea that they can have a role in changing the present and the future. They begin to understand that they can be active participants in the world around them. They can make a difference; they can have a say."

Communicating Your Vision

For Landay, understanding how culture works is especially important for artists. She urges aspiring artists to "develop your own unique voice by being brave about how you see the world. When you see something in a different way, go with that. Do not pull back into what seems to be the way that everyone else sees things."

She also urges artists not to rush. "Sometimes you have to wait until what you see develops into something that you can articulate in a way that others can understand. *That* is where the tools come in. Take your time to learn the tools that you need in order to create. Use the tools in a way so that you can show someone else what you mean, so that they can see it too.

"Sometimes," she acknowledges, "that process of communication can be really frustrating. You see something but you have not figured out how to show it to someone else in a way that they can see it.

"That gap," she explains, "between what we can imagine and what we can actually do in our craft and in our art—that can sometimes seem large. Get better at your craft, at using tools, to close that gap."

She continues, "No one will ever believe how much time it takes you to master a particular technique that will make something work the right way. This can make being an artist really hard. But if all that work gets you a little bit closer to being able to show someone what you have seen, something that they have not seen yet, then it is worth it. Be patient. Trust yourself. And do not be afraid to share your vision."

PART III

Sustaining Culture and Community

Introduction

Part III, Sustaining Culture and Community, explores the role of the artist as a member and leader of his or her community. To be an artist, one must understand the social and cultural environments in which one creates. The artists in the section that follows discuss the ways that their work is affected by and impacts current social issues. Likewise, artists discuss their responsibility to and interaction with the society in which they live.

In Chapter 11, The Politics of Art, Peabody Award-winner and spoken word artist **Bruce George** examines the political nature of art—the ways that art is created in and shapes politics and culture.

In Chapter 12, *New York Times*-bestselling author **Doug Stanton** explores the ways that his work as a writer relates not only to other arts but to the community in which he lives. Stanton's connections with his family and community define him as much as his writing career does. In the small town in which he lives, he is working to build an artist community that benefits everyone and especially young and aspiring artists.

In Chapter 13, director and choreographer **Otis Sallid** explains that studying movement is important for all artists, not only dancers. The study of dance, he believes, is a metaphor for studying oneself and one's culture. According to Sallid, all artists have to push themselves to learn history, culture and politics, and the "languages" of art. "If you speak only one language, you are limiting yourself...Learn the *languages*," he says. "That is what makes great art."

In this section, artists delve into the ways that society shapes artists, and art shapes the society in which we live.

CHAPTER 11

Bruce George

Photo used with permission.

The Politics of Art

Bruce George is a poet, writer, editor, and activist. Born and raised in New York City, he earned a Bachelor of Arts in Psychology from Niagara University.

George is most widely known for co-founding Russell Simmons Presents Def Poetry Jam *on HBO, for which he won a Peabody Award in 1999. He also worked with* Def Poetry Jam on Broadway, *for which he won a Tony.*

He has founded a number of organizations, including Ebony Energy Talent Network—a booking agency for Rev. Jesse Jackson, Amiri Baraka, The Last Poets, and others; the social networking website Ning; and Bone Bristle Entertainment, LLC.

George also works with Gumbo for the Soul Publications, International Hip-Hop Speakers Bureau, Audible, Inc., Step to the Mic, Rebel Poetry Spoken Word, and The American Experiment Peace Project, an anti-violence and poverty initiative.

A former gang member, George is an activist for gang awareness. In 2008, he co-edited, with Louis Reyes Rivera, The Bandana Republic *to help bring gang members into the literary world, and to break some of the stereotypes associated with them.*

In this chapter, George examines the political nature of art and the ways that art is created in and shapes politics and culture.

Art, argues Bruce George, enables people to move beyond themselves, out of the individualistic, and towards the social, connecting with each other and working for some larger good. Art is not about the "I," says George. "It is about the *we*. It is not about the individual. It is about the collective."

To accomplish this journey from the individual to the collective, the artist has to begin with what he or she knows. For George, "One's culture plus experience equals one's frame of reference." The artist re-creates that frame of reference in a way that makes his or her world visible to others. Through one's individual understanding of his or her world, artists help people make connections.

George's poem, "Spiritually Rooted," illustrates these concepts. In the poem, the speaker joins with the listener and becomes more than him or herself alone.

Spiritually Rooted

Without pretense
I walk along your shadow
and introduce my foreground
to your background
and in surround sound
aura's blush
Childlike
while genuflecting to each other
we exchanged one-part watercolor
to two-parts acrylic
became fixtures in spirit
...they can keep our leaves
for we are rooted
irrespective of seasons
and hormones
we keep growing
   and bending
and breathing
   and dressing
and breathing
   and undressing
and breathing
   and bearing
and bearing
   and bearing
fruit!

The speaker is "without pretense" and is walking "along your shadow," joining with the poem's "you." The speaker's "foreground" connects with "your background." Both speaker and listener are respectful—"genuflecting to each other"—exchange "one-part watercolor/to two-parts acrylic," and become something new. This new connection keeps "growing/and bending...and bearing/and bearing/and bearing/fruit." From the union, comes new life—literally or metaphorically.

The beauty of this poem—its focus on romantic and sexual love and also on social connection—reveals George's philosophy and understanding of art. For George, art is "all about fostering a sense of reciprocity, not in the sense that one hand washes the other, that we do things for others so that we receive something in return." That is not what George means. Instead, he believes art helps people identify with others. "Art gives people some kind of social outlook on life." It leads them to care for others.

To be the guides who take people from the individual to the social, artists themselves need to understand their world. For George, this understanding comes through study and lifelong learning. He stresses the importance of reading and of studying literature. He attributes his success as a poet, an artist, a thinker, and a person to his love of reading.

"I read all types of literature," says George, "and I am fascinated with books, because they give you the opportunity to travel all around the world and to experience others' perspectives. They are an inexpensive way to see the world vicariously through the eyes of the writer. They give people the opportunity to step outside of themselves and to compare their own life experiences with those of others.

"I always tell young people to read and to re-read. Some might think that reading is a waste of time, or that they are too busy to read, but artists are well-read people. They understand that they need to make their world as large as possible and that books help them do that."

An Active Activist

Along with reading, George stresses that artists need to be aware of and involved with current events. They need to understand politics and relationships of power and their own attitudes about these relationships. They need to know that they want to do something about the injustices they see in their world.

George emphasizes that he is an "active activist." For him, art and activism are intimately and completely connected. As he explains, "A lot of people have an antiquated view of what an activist is. Usually, when people think about an activist, they think of that person in a very retro way. They think: 60s, revolutionary movement, getting arrested, and raising their fists. But that is not what I mean.

"Activism is fostering change. Art helps to foster change; it helps people to better themselves politically, socially, as well as personally. I use my activism as a way to empower people, to teach people to have more of a sense of self-determination."

George is a religious person and believes that his "mandate from God" has been to minister to people through his art and to foster artistry in others. Art, he believes, can help people escape what he describes as "the mentality of consumption" of modern society. "Society conditions us to focus just on ourselves, to have this individualistic disposition at the expense of the welfare and concern of others. As an activist, I minister to people to become more than they are, to be less self-centered, to focus more on other people, to be less apathetic, to be more caring of others.

"Art," says George, "takes you out of the self and gives you the opportunity to identify with and understand others."

George also believes that one's art and activism continue to evolve. "As an artist," he says, "you cannot retire from art. As an activist, you cannot retire from struggle. You have to continue to study, to reinvent yourself. That is what I am all about."

While as an artist you need to be true to yourself and to focus on what you know, it is also important, argues George, to "tap into a myriad of issues and topics. My writing is diverse in the sense that I write about social and political topics, as well as issues that are personal. I am well aware that all art is political.

"Either your work challenges the status quo or it maintains it. I challenge. My writing addresses political issues in some shape, form, or fashion. I want readers and listeners to get a sense of pride and self-determination from my writing. When you read Langston Hughes, you get a sense of pride. It's about empowerment. I use my art to foster self-esteem and dignity in the African and urban heritage."

Langston Hughes (1902-1967) was an African-American poet, novelist, and playwright, known for his portrayals of black life in America.

George's groundbreaking book, *The Bandana Republic: A Literary Anthology by Gang Members and Their Affiliates* (Softskull Press, 2008), which he co-edited with Louis Reyes Rivera, is a testament to this understanding of art's purpose. The anthology collects moving and powerful works by gang members and ex-gang members. It provides a forum for those without voice to express their ideas, feelings, regrets, and hopes. It also provides a window into a life that many outside of gang culture know about only through stereotypes. Through this artistic sharing, there is a hope for increased understanding.

George explains, "*The Bandana Republic* gives voice to people who come out of street organizations. Gangs are street organizations. I wanted to create a book that dealt with gang literature, because historically some of the best literature and art comes out of the streets. Look at hip hop, for example.

"Also, some of the best art comes out of prisons. Being confined gives some of these artists their first opportunity to become introspective. *The Bandana Republic* was a way to create a platform, so that people who are in street organizations can express themselves in an unfettered fashion. I wanted to show the world that some of the best minds and the best art come from people who were misguided."

George, who is a former gang member, adds, "I overstood—*not* understood—the value of street literature, because I saw firsthand the phenomenal poets and artists who come from the street, who are under-looked or overlooked as a result of where they come from."

Personal Development

George began writing as a child, and throughout his life, his poetry and artistry has helped to keep him grounded. His poetry was very much influenced by his mother.

He explains, "My mother, Elaine George, was always a lover of words. She would use these exotic words around me. As a result, I fell in love with words. In addition, I was raised by my mom alone, an only child in a single parent home. As a result, I became very introspective. I did not have the outlet of a brother or sister around, and so I would become creative in my own way and I would use poetry, or rap, to express myself.

"Often this was an outlet to express my anger, especially when I was a teen, my disillusionment with not having a father around. Through poetry, I would vent my sense of not knowing who I was, confusion, all of those things that young people go through. I was able to use poetry as a way to be able to rescue myself and have an outlet for those pent up feelings."

But poetry was not always enough to rescue George. When he was a teen, he became involved in gangs and was forced to leave Samuel Gompers High School in the Bronx for what was called "inciting a riot." From this devastating experience, George's life took a positive turn. He spent two years in a live-in Job Corps program in Albany, New York, a government-funded education and training program that helps young people earn a high school diploma and prepare for a career. For George, this was a saving grace. "This taught me a skill. It gave me structure. It gave me a chance for self-determination and it gave me a sense of hope."

For the first time in his life, George left New York City. Albany seemed like a completely new and wide world. There, he explains, "I met different people, met peers from different parts of the country, male and female. I was introduced to Islam through The Five Percent Nation.

"When I joined the Five Percenters, this was the ultimate in discipline because you are a servant of God. I had never thought of myself as a servant of anyone. I stopped smoking and drinking—it has been 27 years now. That was instrumental in transforming me. Job Corps gave me a structure, which is what I needed. I became more focused, more centered. With that structure, my learning could begin."

> The Five Percent Nation is an organization whose followers believe in twelve axioms by which one should live: knowledge, wisdom, understanding, freedom, justice, equality, food, clothing, shelter, love, peace, and happiness.

From Job Corps, George went to Niagara University and earned his bachelor's degree. George, no longer a Muslim, now sees himself as "a child of God. Accepting Jesus Christ as my Lord and Savior also helped turn me around. Being a Muslim was important to me when I was a youth, but it did not feel natural to me. God has blessed me to be a Christian."

Slam Poetry and Def Poetry Jam

After college, George returned to New York City with the idea of helping others achieve the kind of focus and self-determination that he had achieved by fostering art and community. In the 1990s, he became involved in the performance poetry and the poetry slam circuit that was thriving in New York and across the country. He won slam contests at some of the city's most competitive performance poetry venues. In 1998 and 1999, he was part of the Brooklyn Moon Café's winning slam teams. In 2003, he was the co-recipient of the Nuyorican Poetry Cafe's First Annual Milky Award for Def Poetry Jam.

In 1999, George says he was "blessed," when he co-founded a forum for performance poetry that has been instrumental in popularizing the art form—HBO's *Def Poetry Jam.*

"I was a spoken word artist at the time, heavily on the circuit. One day I was watching *Def Comedy Jam* on HBO, and I received this epiphany. Here on *Comedy Jam* was a mic, an audience, and a stage. And I thought, 'That is us, but instead of comedy, why not have a Def Poetry Jam?' So I bookmarked that idea, because I did not have a relationship with Russell Simmons, founder of the hip-hop label Def Jam and of HBO's *Def Comedy Jam.* But I kept my eyes and ears open for a chance to talk with him.

"And the chance came. I heard that Danny Simmons, Russell's brother, was doing poetry at his art gallery home. I went there and said to Danny, 'What do you think about a poetry version of *Def Comedy Jam?*' He was receptive. We met with Russell, who understood the power of performance poetry. He saw that in rap you can hide behind the music, but that when you take the music away, you have to make sense. He saw this as a viable art form and a new art form, and he was excited about it."

Russell Simmons (1957-) is an American entrepreneur who co-founded—with Rick Rubin—the music label Def Jam Recordings in 1984.

In large part due to the success of *Def Poetry Jam* on HBO, performance poetry, once a coffee house art form, has become a viable commercial and popular endeavor. Poetry has moved from the local venue to the television—from coffee shop, bar, and school to everyone's living room.

Some of the poets, says George, "were concerned that performance poetry would lose its 'purity,' because of this popularization and commercialization." But, he explains, "all art forms start out on the side stream, very pure, very virgin like, very true to their essence. Then they segue to the mainstream. When an art gets more into the mainstream, and money people get involved, it becomes more tainted and more compromised. Every art form goes through that bastardization process, and yet you are always going to have certain individuals who are going to remain true to that art form."

George continues, "I tell individual artists: Don't worry about an art form becoming bastardized. It is not about the art form. It is all about you. Stay true to your art. As an individual, your moral compass should be headed in the right direction in terms of where you see your art going. If you are listening to hip hop and the words are misogynistic, don't buy it and don't support it. Either you are part of the problem or part of solution."

This reveals George's philosophy that art is, by its nature, political. It is about building a community of connected individuals. If artists focus only on their individual success and bend to what they think is popular or commercial, argues George, then they are part of the problem. If they stay true to themselves and the work of art, then they are part of the solution.

Those who become part of the problem are not guaranteed any more commercial success than those who remain true to themselves. In fact, George believes strongly that the most successful artists—those who are able to make a living at their art and who have platforms to express themselves—are those who are most honest about their work and are true to their own moral sense.

George adds, "All artists need to understand or overstand how important it is to be true to yourself and not let others define you. Artists need to overstand that they are a brand, that they have to protect their brand, their reputation, their image. As they become greater and greater artists, they are constantly being judged. They're constantly under the spotlight, so they have to watch how they move, how they speak."

Becoming Saleable without Selling Out

George's advice to aspiring artists emphasizes that "artists have to make themselves saleable without selling out.

"I want to underscore that," he says. "Without compromising your values, without compromising your morals, you have to overstand the fact that you are a brand, that your name is a brand, that your image is a brand, and that you have a lot to offer people.

"People are willing to buy into that, if you have the right attitude. If you have the wrong attitude, if you are only about the money, then doors will continue to close. It is about having the right attitude and being open and taking care of your body. It is about drinking and eating properly, taking care of your physical and mental health and your well being, so you can be a better artist, a more effective artist. That is what it is all about."

George himself has had much commercial success and wants to use his success to help others. "A goal of mine is to create platforms for other artists to free themselves from corporate America, to free people from having to work for someone else, to be able to support themselves with their art."

Because of his work with *Def Poetry Jam* , and the growth of a commercial poetry market—in terms of books, performances, college presentations—hundreds of poets today are able to do what many poets in past generations could not do so easily: give up their day jobs and earn a living from their poetry.

George explains that another goal of his "is to become the world's first literary mogul." He laughs. "When people hear the word 'mogul,' it usually has the connotation of someone with a lot of money. That is a myopic way of looking at the word. A mogul is a relationship expert, a portal. I want to be an urban portal where I can get information, feed information, connect people. If you want to learn how to write a book, I got you. If you need a publisher, I got you. My goal is to assist people in being writers, in being published, in resolving their jobs and replacing those jobs with a career, to liberate people from their '9 to 5.'"

"When I lead workshops," continues George, "I teach people that part of the creative process is to be true to who you are, to create what you know. Be true to your voice. Believe in yourself. And, always think about your next level. If you do this, you will be able to develop as an artist and as a person."

CHAPTER 12

Doug Stanton

Photo used with permission.

Writing and Living in the Community

Doug Stanton is the author of the New York Times *bestsellers* In Harm's Way: The Sinking of the U.S.S. Indianapolis and the Extraordinary Story of Its Survivors *and* Horse Soldiers: The Extraordinary Story of a Band of U.S. Soldiers Who Rode to Victory in Afghanistan.

In Harm's Way *was chosen as a* New York Review of Books Best Books in Print 2001, *a* Publishers Weekly *Notable Book of 2001, and a Michigan Notable Book of the Year. It was a finalist for the WH Smith Award in the UK and the Great Lakes Book Festival Best Book Award.*

Stanton has appeared on NBC Nightly News *and made multiple appearances on CNN, FOX,* The History Channel, *Imus in the Morning, A&E, and C-SPAN's* BookTV. *His writing about the U.S. military has appeared in the* New York Times Book Review *and* The Washington Post.

A former contributing editor at Esquire, Sports Afield, *and* Outside, *Stanton is now a contributing editor at* Men's Journal *and has written extensively on travel, adventure, entertainment, and politics.*

Stanton lives in his hometown of Traverse City, Michigan, where he is active as a member of the advisory board of the Interlochen Center for The Arts Motion Picture Arts program, a board of trustees member of The Pathfinder School, and a founder of the National Writers Series, a year-round book festival, whose scholarship program seeks to inspire young authors wishing to study writing in college.

Stanton graduated from Interlochen and earned a Bachelor of Arts from Hampshire College. He also earned a Master of Fine Arts from the University of Iowa Writers' Workshop, where he studied both poetry and fiction.

In this chapter, Stanton explores the ways that artists build community.

With two bestselling nonfiction books and a successful journalism career, Doug Stanton works full time as a writer. He is also a community member, a husband, a father, and a son. His connections with his family and his community define him as much, if not more, than his writing career.

Stanton grew up in Traverse City, located on Grand Traverse Bay in Michigan's northern lower peninsula. The city of fifteen thousand people is the major commercial center in mostly rural northern Michigan, and it is the largest producer of tart cherries in the United States.

Stanton purchased the modest house next door to the one where he lives with his family to serve as his writing studio. His computer sits on a high table, so that he is able to write while standing. "That is easier for me," he says. Stacks of books sit on chairs, benches, and the floor.

"Sometimes," says Stanton, "I will just print pages of notes and tape them to the walls. Then I can organize and sort and make decisions about the writing." His writing process involves conducting hours of interviews and collecting dozens of details. He sorts through transcripts to find the narrative pulse and carves the story from inside the notes—to uncover the heart of what motivates the key players being presented.

Stanton always knew that he wanted to write. This essential part of his identity has shaped his goals since he was a boy. For Stanton, identity and community are closely connected. In his writing, he focuses on how individuals define themselves, what drives them, and their own sense of personhood and integrity. He also focuses on how communities shape, foster, and support individuals. These themes are also important in his life.

Stanton took a very deliberate path to wind up where he is today, writing in the community that he loves, where he was raised, living in the way he wants. Figuring out how to have a successful writing career while also living in small town America was something of a challenge.

Stanton credits the education he received from Interlochen with his start in writing. He is also extremely grateful to his friend and mentor, Jim Harrison, another national writer who lives and works out of Traverse City, for serving as a role model and helping Doug make connections in the industry. As he has achieved success, Stanton founded the National Writers Series, bringing established authors to Traverse City and offering scholarships to aspiring writers.

Jim Harrison (1937-) is an American author known for his poetry, fiction, and essays. His novels include *Legends of the Fall* and *Dalva*.

Terry McDonell (1944-), a novelist and screenwriter, has headed the Sports Illustrated Group since 2006.

Stanton wants to do for young people what was done for him as a boy. He recalls, "My parents were very supportive of my writing. By the age of fourteen, I knew that I liked to write. I was sitting in eighth grade journalism class at the junior high school. The teacher asked if anyone knew about the new writing program at Interlochen. I didn't, but my hand shot up, and I said that I would like to go there.

"My teacher encouraged me to apply. I did and was accepted. The program was as good or better than any first two years of college. They took things very seriously. They had writers come in. When you are fourteen, it was very heady and very important. I went there in ninth grade. We couldn't afford to send me in tenth grade. So I left and went to the public high school. I got a job and saved the bulk of the money for half of eleventh grade and most of twelfth grade, but it was not quite enough, and a local woman gave me the extra $1,000 that I needed. I never forgot that, because it was the money I needed to keep going.

"Around this same time, when I was a student at Interlochen, I first met Jim Harrison. I had read his books. This was a transformative moment. If you are holding a book as a young student or holding a sheet of music or a recording for music students, you wonder: 'How did this object come into being?' It really could just as easily exist in another galaxy as far as you are concerned. You are holding it, but have no idea how it was formed.

"But when I would walk down the street and see Jim Harrison in a local restaurant, the distance between that book and me was no longer a galaxy but it was literally ten feet. I would talk with him. I understood probably three percent of what he was saying, but it didn't matter, because then I could see, 'Oh, I can get from here to there.' I could get from being me to having my own book. Because here was this guy, living and breathing in the same existential plane as I was, and he had done it.

"Receiving the money and seeing a famous writer here in Traverse City were two transformative experiences. The National Writers Series is meant to do the same thing for other young people.

"I am convinced that some of these students are going to write the next *The Sun Also Rises*. And I will be pleased to help those young people achieve their goals and create the art that we need in our world today."

Stanton's Artistic Journey

"I wrote from an early age," Stanton explains. He was writing poems as a high school student and as an undergraduate. At Iowa, he entered the poetry workshop and then transferred to fiction. He explains, "I thought I would just write and teach. I did not worry very much about how to make a living."

After receiving his Master of Fine Arts from Iowa, Stanton looked for a job teaching. "I didn't know if it would be easy or hard to get a job. It turns out that it was hard. I sent out sixty job applications and received one response—from Northeast Louisiana University, which is now the University of Louisiana at Monroe. There were some people there who created a good, vibrant English department. They had writers come in. They were receptive to poets. I taught five sections of college composition a semester. I liked teaching a lot, but after two years, I saw that I really couldn't keep up this pace. It would be a while before I got a teaching load that would allow me to write."

Stanton realized after he was working in Louisiana that he needed to direct his career more fully, or as he says, "worry a little more, have a plan."

A turning point came when Stanton returned to Traverse City for his break between semesters. "I was at a bar on New Year's Eve when I ran into Jim Harrison." Stanton again asked Harrison for advice. "I said that I needed to move back to Traverse City and become a writer. But I did not know how I would make a living. He said to me, 'Well, it is easy. Just start writing nonfiction.'"

Stanton had not considered nonfiction before. He had written poetry and short stories but was not yet a journalist. Harrison encouraged him and offered him help. "He told me to send him something and he would see if he could send it to an editor in New York.

"So I went back to Louisiana and worked very hard on this long essay. I had no idea how to write a saleable piece for a mass market. I had no idea what magazine journalism was. I worked and worked on it and worked on it some more. Then I sent it to Jim."

Harrison sent Stanton's piece to a friend, Terry McDonell, who is now the editor-in-chief of the Sports Illustrated Group. "At the time," continues Stanton, "Terry was running this magazine called *Smart*. He had worked at *Newsweek* and *Rolling Stone*. He had been an editor of Hunter Thompson. He is one of the last great magazine editors in New York, and he ran magazines when magazines really meant something.

"Terry told Jim, 'I can't publish this, but send me something else.'"

Stanton took that challenge. He wrote a short piece about proposing marriage to his wife, Anne. McDonell published this essay, called 'Marry Me, Marry Me,' in the May 1990 *Smart*, and paid Stanton $1,700 for 1,700 words. "I thought, 'Wow, this is easy. I am on my way,'" he remembers.

"Then, Anne and I were married in June 1990. On our receiving line, Jim Harrison gave us a check for $500 with a note with a name on it, Ric Bohy, then editor of *Detroit Monthly*. Ric gave me my first real magazine assignment. So I moved back to Traverse City. I wrote that piece for Ric. And I hustled and wrote whatever I could."

Soon McDonell became editor of *Esquire* magazine and brought Harrison with him. This connection was important for Stanton. He explains, "I was writing articles for local magazines in Traverse City, trying to make ends meet. By chance, I saw an advertisement for a men's retreat, inspired by Robert Bly's book, *Iron John*. All over America, guys were going on these weekend retreats. I proposed to Terry that I attend one of these and write about it. I did, and the article got a lot of play."

Robert Bly (1926-) is an American author and poet whose book *Iron John* is credited for starting the Mythopoetic Men's Movement in the U.S.

Learning to Write—Again

That article was a success. But writing it, Stanton says, "was a whole other story. It was hard, especially since I had no real journalism training." His wife, Anne, now an investigative reporter with *Northern Express Magazine*, a northwest Michigan newsweekly, helped him. "Anne had been a journalism major at the University of Michigan, so I asked her how to do interviews. I really had to teach myself how to be a reporter."

An important "textbook" for Stanton, instrumental to his self-education, was *Smiling through the Apocalypse:* Esquire's *History of the Sixties*, published

> *Smiling through the Apocalypse: Esquire's History of the Sixties* was a collection of essays whose contributors included James Baldwin, Saul Bellow, Norman Mailer, Gore Vidal, and Tom Wolfe.

in 1987.[1] It was a collection of some of the most important stories *Esquire* published in the 1960s. The stories were written in the style that came to be known as "new journalism," a kind of nonfiction writing where the journalist uses fiction-writing techniques to capture the sense of place and time. For Stanton, educated as a fiction writer, learning to transfer his writing style to the nonfiction world was key to his success.

"When the articles in *Smiling through the Apocalypse* were first published," says Stanton, "they really mattered. This is really excellent writing, by writers like

> Norman Mailer (1923-2007) was a Pulitzer prize winning-writer who helped to develop a new literary genre—creative non-fiction—which combined narrative writing and journalism.

Norman Mailer, Gore Vidal, Tom Wolfe, Gay Talese. I recommend this book to all writing students."

He refers to the piece "Frank Sinatra Has a Cold," by Talese, published in *Esquire* in 1966. "The opening paragraph is all third person omniscient narrator," says Stanton. "Talese isn't in the piece, which is very different from most journalism today, which uses a lot of first person narration. But Talese gains his omniscience by reporting the story. The setting, the details are so real. You, as the reader, feel you are there with Sinatra. You think Talese must be there, too. But then, as I read interviews with Talese about this article, I discovered that he never really interviewed Sinatra. Instead, he interviewed 100 people who knew Sinatra. I thought, this is amazing."

Stanton saw Talese as the kind of writer to which he would aspire. He wanted to learn to write using the techniques Talese used, to make the story come to life. Says Stanton, "I reverse engineered the whole piece. I took that first paragraph and thought, 'What questions did Talese have to ask in order to elicit those details?', because that is what a story is built on, the power of its details. And then I made a list of those questions. Who would he have had to interview to get this information? So that is how I figured out how you report.

"Everything you need to know about great journalism is in that piece."

Being and Doing

Stanton explains, "I have an epigraph by Epictetus at the beginning of *In Harm's Way* which says, 'First say to yourself what would you be, then do what you have to do.' I always was attracted to that quotation, because it sums it all up.

"If you were to wake up and it was the end of the world, literally, or your boat had sunk or if you had been dropped into the middle of enemy-controlled territory during wartime, what would you do? When you wake up on that morning, how are you going to respond and then what are you going to do?"

Stanton pursues this question in his book *In Harm's Way*. How do the survivors of a WWII battleship, torpedoed by a Japanese submarine and left to sink, manage to survive in the water for nearly five days? For Stanton, answering questions like these is what writing is all about. He believes that this connects to what he learned as an undergraduate at Hampshire College.

"Hampshire is very strong on teaching students how to ask questions to solve a problem. In education, if you can instill in a student a sense of curiosity and a sense of being comfortable with terror, then you are successful. By 'terror,' I mean helping students understand how it feels to be in the middle of chaos in a fluid environment, helping them figure out how to think moment-by-moment, how to make rapid decisions, how to find meaning in what they see around them.

"This is what a reporter does, as he or she tries to shape a story. If a school can teach students this skill, well, that is as important as having to remember all the facts of 19th century art history or anything else."

Finding Meaning from Chaos and Terror

Stanton always wanted to write a book, one of his goals since childhood. In 1999, he began to make that goal a reality when he discovered the story of the sinking of the U.S.S. Indianapolis in World War II.

The Indianapolis was a heavy cruiser. On July 26, 1945, it delivered its cargo, the uranium that would be dropped on Hiroshima. Three days later, after leaving the port at the Pacific island of Tinian, on its way to Guam, the ship was torpedoed and sunk in the Pacific Ocean. Three hundred sailors were killed instantly; close to nine hundred were cast into the ocean; three hundred and seventeen would manage to survive.

Captain Charles McVay III was, according to many accounts and persuasively presented by Stanton, unfairly and wrongly blamed for the incident and court-martialed. His sailors objected and in the year 2000, by an act of Congress, he was exonerated. But this came too late for McVay, who killed himself in 1968. Stanton captures the whole drama, especially focusing on the survivors who managed to keep themselves alive while bobbing in the Pacific Ocean for days.

"My editor, Sid Evans," Stanton explains, "called me one day and said, 'You should go to Indianapolis and meet these survivors at a reunion. I did not know much about the story. The movie *Jaws* includes a famous scene that mentions The U.S.S. *Indianapolis* as a disaster at sea. The crazy captain, Robert Shaw, is obsessed with killing sharks. He is a fictional survivor of this disaster. That is all I knew about the *Indianapolis*. But Sid told me, 'The people exist, and you should go down and meet them.' So I did.

"At the hotel, there were sixty survivors and maybe one hundred-twenty grandchildren, children, and wives. It was very much like any family reunion in the Midwest, with laughter and all kinds of innocent banter. But when I asked one of the survivors, Mike Kuryla, who has since passed away, what happened to him in the sinking, he began to tell me a very riveting story which brought me to tears and was very emotional for him to relive. What interested me was that feeling that this moment evoked for him, more than fifty years later.

"I wrote a story, 30,000 words, and *Men's Journal* published 13,000 words. I figured that I had about one-third of a book done. After I turned it in, I thought: I want to do more of this. There was very little existing in writing on these guys. There were three books that focused on the court martial of the captain as a legal drama.

"But, what really interested me was how this event had affected the survivors, Mike Kuryla and other sailors, how they had survived and managed to return to normal life. No one had ever asked Mike how he had managed to move through this experience. That is what interested me as a writer."

Continues Stanton, "The magazine articles that I had been writing at that time were about all kinds of things. I had a facility for the celebrity profile, which I got pretty good at. I tried to make them not fluff pieces, but instead like little short stories about the person. I wrote about George Clooney, Woody Harrelson, and Harrison Ford. It was interesting. It was fun. I enjoyed it, and it paid the bills. I was out traveling. But I was writing the kind of pieces that people read in twenty minutes at O'Hare airport.

"After writing the *Indianapolis* piece," he says, "I felt that I had a stronger purpose. I stopped working on magazine stuff except for occasionally. You know a magazine piece is like a sprint but a book is a long, long journey." Stanton wanted to take that journey.

"Writing the *Indianapolis* book was a much deeper, more meaningful story. That story is about community. It is about will. It is like a mountaineering story, with people battling nature or trying to survive. But it was also deeply personal. Once the book came out, I did a book tour, and it was very moving."

As he went around the country to different book readings, Stanton invited the survivors to come with him and tell their stories. A common theme emerged as they each told their accounts: They remembered being named. Their strong sense of identity kept them, as individuals, from giving up. And their strong sense of community led them to help each other.

Stanton explains. "Dick Thelen, who came to a reading in Ann Arbor, remembered that on the third day of this five-day ordeal, a lot of guys just gave up and started swimming away from the group. He thought about doing that but he didn't. He recalled that one reason he did not was that he heard this voice. It wasn't a voice from God. In Dick's case, it was his dad, saying the thing he always said to him, 'Don't give up.'

"Another survivor, Ed Brown, recalled his father saying to him, 'You are Ed Brown. You don't quit football practice.' That was important for Ed, because that is what he hung on to. If he didn't quit football practice, he wouldn't quit this either.

"Other survivors had a similar experience of hearing a voice. The things that these guys remembered weren't deep philosophical moments. They were just moments when they had been identified or pointed at or named. They recalled words from their fathers, their grandfathers, their mothers, times when they were told, 'You are this. You are that.'

"It made me realize," says Stanton, "that it is really important for young people to have these moments of being given an identity. That is why I thought that the book actually was successful, too, because people understood in the end that the book was about being identified, and it was about being a part of a community."

Individuals survived because they understood themselves, and the group survived because it functioned as a community. For Stanton, these ideas of identity and community, ideas that shape his own understanding of himself, prevail in his writing. The soldiers who survived were strong as individuals. Says Stanton, "A lot of these guys just would not give up. They would not quit. They would do whatever they could to survive. They were survivors."

They also maintained a strong community, even in the middle of the ocean. "If you were floating in the water," says Stanton, "you might swim over to me and put me up on your hip and dog paddle and hold me up for a bit, to give me a break. Then you would get exhausted and swim away. And then I might come and do the same thing for you. And just to keep doing that for what at the time must have seemed like it would be for infinity, like this would just go on forever, this is powerful.

"The determination, the community—that is what made that book so meaningful. The story connected with a lot of people, especially women in their thirties and forties, women whose grandfathers or fathers had been in the war but had never talked about it. They made some associative leaps from this experience to what their own older male members of their family might have gone through but never discussed."

Another War—A Second Book

After the success of his first book, Stanton wondered if he could approach a contemporary war in the same way, as a story of survival "not in a weapons and shooting sort of way, but in the way of figuring out what is going on here." He set out to investigate what was happening in Afghanistan. Who were these U.S. soldiers going on horseback to this unchartered and very risky area? What were they trying to accomplish?

Stanton's second book—*Horse Soldiers: The Extraordinary Story of a Band of U.S. Soldiers Who Rode to Victory in Afghanistan*—took him five years to write, more than twice as long as *In Harm's Way*.

Stanton attributes this to two causes.

First, it was hard to find people to interview. "I thought interviewing people would be easy," says Stanton, "because when I was writing *In Harm's Way*, I would call people, and they would pick up the phone and talk with me. So I figured that I would just call who I needed to talk to, and they will pick up the phone. But it turns out that the people I wanted to talk to were still actively deployed around the world."

Second, and perhaps even more important, Stanton had to start *Horse Soldiers* twice. "I wrote about 150,000 words which I threw out. The first draft had too many people. It was too detailed. It didn't have focus and narrative drive. It didn't capture what I found interesting about the story. I wanted my focus to be the mental agility of the people involved. Their job was to go to this country and not get killed and try to create social change. Their job is to get these people to stop fighting. And their job is to push the Taliban out of the country.

"This was a very different take on the military than I was aware of. I have never been in the army or in the armed services. I thought: Who are these guys? I was fascinated by their calm, how they had so little information and yet were so confident that they would just be able to handle everything when they got there."

When Stanton met the soldiers he features in this book—soldiers belonging to the U.S. Special Forces—he found each of them to be fascinating. As Stanton describes them, "They live under authority, but they're the guys who are happy in a free flowing environment where they have to figure out what to do without anyone telling them.

"If you were to describe them as painters, watching them talk about how they assess the situation, it would be like watching Jackson Pollock paint. They are much more improvisational in their approach, and their training is all designed to allow them to be comfortable in that environment. This involved a lot of creativity."

Artists' Responsibility in Wartime

For Stanton, *Horse Soldiers* was "a bigger and more ambitious book than *In Harm's Way*." He wanted to get across the point of view of the U.S. soldiers and of the Afghans. He explains, "I wanted more omniscience. If I described the Americans walking down a road, I wanted to be able to describe the Afghans, too. I wanted to do enough reporting, so that I could know what the Afghans were thinking. That was the reporting challenging, the writing challenge.

"I wanted to create a story that if you read it, you would unknowingly be digesting this whole kind of worldview about conflict resolution which has to do with cultural awareness, speaking the language, being aware of the aims and goals of the other culture."

Stanton says that he did not overtly choose the subject for his book thinking that he had a political message. However, the book has become political, and Stanton has been called on to comment on the situation in Afghanistan.

Stanton believes that, "If you are going to create peace, you have to study war. If you don't understand why someone else is fighting and how they are fighting, then you don't understand them."

Stanton considers himself "staunchly anti-war. War is one of the most pressing subjects of our time. More writers and artists really need to go elbow-deep into this subject and figure out what it is about, because if we don't, then other people who have a vested economic interest in continuing war are certainly already there figuring out what is going on.

"There is violence in the world, and we need to do something to confront it and end it. Simply walking away is a bit like coming home, finding your house on fire, and saying that you don't believe in fire.

Kurt Vonnegut (1922-2007) was an American writer whose novels included *Cat's Cradle*, *Breakfast of Champions*, and *Slaughterhouse-Five*.

J.D. Salinger (1919-2010), born Jerome David Salinger, was a novelist and short-story writer. His novel *The Catcher in the Rye* has sold more than 60 million copies.

Marcel Duchamp (1887-1968) was a French artist who sought to subvert more traditional art, attracting the viewer through irony and humor.

e.e. cummings, born Edward Estlin Cummings (1894-1962), was an American author, whose poems feature unconventional capitalization and punctuation.

"Look at World War II writers," says Stanton. "Mailer. Vonnegut. Even J.D. Salinger. This question of violence on a global scale really informed the WWII generation of writers. If you read *Catcher in the Rye* and you know that J.D. Salinger was at D-day, there is a sense of futility in that narrative voice that the war informed.

"Or go farther back to World War I," says Stanton. "Look at how Picasso created paintings in which there is no ordering principle. Duchamp was hanging his bicycle seat in the armory show calling it art. ee cummings was writing his poems and not capitalizing anything. There was this great Teutonic shift in the politics of the world and it informed art. But we, as artists today, are so divorced from doing that. That is one of the reasons that I wrote *Horse Soldiers*. Artists need to engage with the war that is impacting all of our lives."

Of the World and of His Small Town

As Stanton discusses the role of artists in today's world, he is also rethinking his own work as an artist, what he wants to say about his life and the world in which he lives. He reflects that his writing, to date, has "not really drawn on his personal life, his reservoir of memory and experience." He is becoming more interested in writing about his life, his story, his experiences in small town America and in Traverse City. "There is not a lot of hoopla here," he says, "and I like it that way." For Stanton, there is a message here—an idea about community, about the past and the future, about the best way to live—that he would like to explore.

He began this exploration with an essay he wrote for the *New York Times* on August 4, 2010, "What the River Dragged In."[2] The essay discusses an oil spill in Michigan's Kalamazoo River, a river which empties into Lake Michigan. Unlike his usual omniscient style, Stanton wrote this in first person and put himself in the piece—the swimmer who enjoys Lake Michigan and may experience the damage of the spill.

> "So for now, I swim. Winters are so long in northern Michigan, nearly nine months of gray skies and deep snow, that summer comes as a fresh burst. Amnesia sets in—you forget that winter will ever return. Friends from other parts of the country descend. The days ripen perfectly, the air no warmer or colder than your skin, so that the edges of your body seem to extend beyond you, up and down the tree-lined streets.
>
> Traverse City sits halfway between the North Pole and the Equator, and our summer days are long. The light seems to take forever to vanish from the sky and, when it does, it goes out like someone folding a white sheet in the dark. A flare on the horizon. Then a rustle: Goodnight.
>
> I swim in the midst of bad news to stay sane. I crawl over the sand bottom in six feet of water, which is cold and green, and nothing has changed in my life—I'm a kid again."

This essay, which Stanton says, "I wrote in two hours on deadline, very loose and very easy," garnered a tremendous amount of email. Around the same time, he wrote an article about the U.S. detention facility in Parwan province, just north of Kabul, for *Time* magazine. Says Stanton, "Three point six million people read that. I don't think I got a single email. That is a much more straightforward reported piece. The one in the *New York Times* is a lot more idiosyncratic, and it connected with more people."

Stanton believes that you should leave the world with more than you took away. This philosophy has inspired his community service work, his work with the National Writer Series, and his work with local school boards. He would like this philosophy also to enter his own writing.

As he determines the subject for his next book, he knows that it will deal with the strange and violent times in which we live, and will suggest a way out. He envisions a literary work that somehow "creates a tonality or a sense of narrative in a world that seems to be extremely bifurcated, atonal, and not rhyming in any sense of the word."

He hasn't yet determined the shape of that work, but he knows that he will.

Notes

1. Hayes, Harold. *Smiling through the Apocalypse: Esquire's History of the Sixties.* NY: An Esquire Press Book, Crown Publishers, 1987. Print.

2. Stanton, Doug. "What the River Dragged In." *Nytimes.com.* 4 Aug. 2010. Web. 4 Aug. 2010.

CHAPTER 13

Otis Sallid

Photo used with permission.

The Languages of Art

Otis Sallid is a dancer, choreographer, director, and producer in theater, television, and film. Among his many projects, he choreographed Spike Lee's School Daze, Do the Right Thing, *and* Malcolm X. *He worked with Thomas Carter on* Swing Kids, *and he worked on the television shows* Living Single *and* Suddenly Susan. *He has choreographed the Academy Awards and the Super Bowl and has produced commercials for Ford, General Motors, Coca Cola, Sprite, and McDonald's.*

His theater credits are also numerous. He conceived of the Broadway show Smokey Joe's Café, *wrote* Spiritual, *a musical that looks at Negro spirituals, and he wrote the plays* Gospel! Gospel! Gospel!, Big Otis Jump Up Blues Revue, *and* Mancini.

Winner of the prestigious Bob Fosse L.A. Choreographer Dance Award, Sallid attended the High School of Performing Arts in New York City, as well as The Juilliard School. He has studied with Martha Graham, Antony Tudor, and Alvin Ailey.

He currently teaches at the Philadelphia Dance Company's summer intensive program and at Berklee College of Music's Stage Performance summer workshop. He runs his own production company, CreativeOtis, and he serves as Performing Arts Co-Director for the Champs Charter High School of the Arts in Van Nuys, California.

In this chapter, Sallid explains how important it is for artists to learn the many different languages of art and to understand the power they have to shape and influence culture. Sallid is especially dedicated to using his art to tell truths about racial identity in the United States.

Otis Sallid carries himself with a dancer's style. The movement by which he places his coffee cup on the table has a certain grace that the simple gesture lacks in most of us. Still, he does not define himself primarily as a dancer. He calls himself a "creative." Sallid does not want to classify himself or his art by putting just one label on it. He sees himself as the creative person who can help others pull their ideas and concepts together. "This is why my company is CreativeOtis," he explains.

"I don't define myself as just a dancer or a producer. That puts boxes around what I do and doesn't enable me to be fully who I am," he says. "The bigger box—the creative box—is really open. I am always looking out, expanding, adding. I look at what I want to do and just go after it."

He explains how learning to work with film helped expand him artistically. "When I was working for Warner Bros. and Sony, when I learned how to shoot film, I realized that you can't have any kind of boundaries around you. Film is expansive, and you have to be ready to expand."

He adds a qualifier, "It is important to know your art well, to fully master it, as you also try to change it, break beyond the boundaries, and make it your own."

Connections: Speaking the Language of Art

Sallid emphasizes connections among the arts and stresses the importance of understanding art's "language." The best artists are communicating and connecting with their art, and they understand that different art forms are linked.

"For example," says Sallid, "dance is music. Music is dance. There is no real difference between them. People make that mistake. There is no difference, so the music devices are the same as dance devices. The way you choreograph is the way you create music. It is the same exact thing. For example, in music there is theme and variation. This is the same thing in dance. Once you really get it, you can just open up with what you are trying to create."

He adds, "Every musician should consider the study of dance and dance history as a way of being informed as to what he or she is playing or singing. How can you know or play the rumba, merengue, samba, or cha cha, without ever experiencing them? In the European classical idiom, one needs to see and know the minuet, gigue, gavotte, pavane, galliard, and courante, as well as the waltz and polka. The music for many of these grew from the dances."

For Sallid, connections become clear, when we realize that all art is about communication and language. Great art—great music, for example—Sallid explains, "is not necessarily about the thing itself. Yes, it is important to hit the notes but equally as important to awaken the spirit, to pay attention to the overall feeling and heart of the composition.

"Much of music is virtually impossible to understand without knowing dance. Dance contains the sub-text and emotional underpinnings of music. Music and dance do not really function without the other."

He recalls, "I will never forget the moment in the middle of filming *Malcolm X*, the movie, that I had to inform the musicians that if they were not with the dancers, then 'they ain't swingin'.' The same thing is true for the dancers. If they are not listening and riding the music, 'they ain't swingin'.

"Many times, it is about seeing if you can speak the language. Can you tell the listeners what you want them to hear? Are you astute enough and clear enough in your language to say what you mean?

"In that way, I've learned that art is really about language and communication and not about dance or music. Can I, through dance and music, through my art, can I get you to feel what I want you to feel? Can I make you laugh? Can I make you cry? Can I make you feel jealous? Can you get the intricacies and the finite elements of what I am trying to tell you? Can I reach my desired goal? If I can, then I have a certain command of the language. I have to be clear as an artist about what I am trying to tell you for you to get it. I have to be clear musically, choreographically, dramatically."

For Sallid, art involves creating an empathic connection with the audience and moving the audience emotionally. It is also about telling a story that the audience cares about and understands. Stage performance—whether it is a musical performance, a dance performance, or a theatrical performance—involves the performer sharing his or her self-understanding with the audience.

The performer, says Sallid, "understands the who, what, and where" of the performance—"who he is, what he is doing, and where he is." The successful performer—clear about his or her own intentionality—communicates this to the audience and moves the audience to a new insight.

Sallid explains, "So, in a way, it doesn't really matter how good you are as a dancer or how good you are as a musician. What matters: Do you understand yourself and your purpose, and can you communicate that understanding? There have been many choreographers who are not great dancers, but they can choreograph well. They communicate. There have been many musicians who are not great musicians, but they know who they are and how to connect with the audience, and in that, they are great artists.

"I have learned," adds Sallid, "that everything is connected. Nothing is disconnected. I do not believe that you can be a thief on one side of your life and a great musician on another and that those two sides can stay separate. What you do in the dark will come to light.

"When you speak the language of art, you are always telling truths about who you are, and that is what people want to know and feel—your truth.

"Art is not about being famous. It is about communicating, being honest."

Personal and Artistic Mentors

Sallid points to a number of people who have helped him learn the language of connection and notes that many of them were women. "The women in my life made me understand things more deeply." They helped him develop as an artist by enabling him to see what was most important. He explains, "From them, I learned how to look at art, how to have the power of discernment. I learned to have faith and to see things through. Women taught me that." He references his mother, his wife, and teachers who were women.

"Each time I crossed genres," he says, "there was always somebody who made a difference and, for me, it was always a woman, not a love interest but a clairvoyant, someone who said, 'Oh, this will be a good move.'

"When I went into television, for instance, it was Debbie Allen. She taught me everything."

Debbie Allen (1950-) is a two-time Emmy award-winning American actress, dancer, choreographer, and director.

"That it was always a woman helping me, that is pretty big," he says. "But I also mean something bigger than this: It is your woman side that helps you as an artist and helps you understand what is important.

"Every man has a woman side, and every woman should have a man side. Your woman side is what you call on to see those higher and intuitive powers. Your woman side is what you call on to make sure that there is survival of the human race."

"Those qualities are great qualities in an artist. To negate your woman side, for an artist, for anyone, really, is foolish. You are missing the legs to your arms.

"It wasn't until I understood the whole female side of my work that artistry really came to light for me," he adds. "A lot of the female side of my work goes unspoken. I think of it like this, like the way that women can look at each other across the room and just get what they are talking about, and no words are spoken. It is a different kind of communication. Most people have this. To not have it and to not recognize it is a shame."

One Foot in the Classroom and One Foot in the Hood

Sallid discusses his childhood and the impact his mother had upon him, how she helped him appreciate his "woman side."

"We grew up in a welfare hotel," he recalls, "in the 1950s and 1960s. And welfare hotels in Harlem back then are not like they are now. There were fifteen beds on one side of the room and fifteen on the other side and a hot plate underneath. Your mother had to get you up and get you to whatever school you could get to. And so you would decide whether you were going to walk to school and have your fifteen cents for lunch. Times were really tough. And Harlem was a different place then.

"We were proud. You could walk down the street and literally, you could see Miles Davis. You could see John Coltrane and Adam Clayton Powell.

"I could see Langston Hughes on my block. James Baldwin went to my school. He lived around the corner. LeRoi Jones. Nat Hentoff. It was a wonderful time to grow up in Harlem. It was very literary. Nikki Giovanni would hang out on the corner. I mean this was my world.

"Growing up, when I got into the High School of the Performing Arts, that was a big, big, big, big deal. We believed in education. My family is from St. Kitts in the Caribbean. They are West Indian and are hardworking. For them, you gotta have an education and seven jobs." He laughs.

"Harlem in the 1950s and 1960s was a wonderful place to be. We were getting an education like no other education. So I always said that I had one foot in the classroom and one foot in the hood. And that somewhat represents my art.

"I am a classical artist who is from the hood. I have never lost my African-American sensibility—we called it 'Negro' then—and I don't think I ever will. I am always reaching for those stories—stories of America's racial past—to be told. Through my art, I always want to see who we are, not only Black people but I am talking about America, through my lens, which is very different from how others might see it.

Miles Davis (1926-1991) was an American jazz trumpet player, composer, and bandleader, and one of the most influential musicians of the 20th century.

John Coltrane (1926-1967) was an American jazz saxophonist, composer, and musical innovator, whose albums include *My Favorite Things* and *A Love Supreme*.

Adam Clayton Powell, Jr., (1908-1972) was a New York pastor, civil rights leader, and politician who became chairman of the Education and Labor Committee in 1961.

Nat Hentoff (1925-) is an American author, journalist, and country and jazz music critic. He is also known for his political writings on free speech and the First Amendment.

James Baldwin (1924-1987) was an African-American author, whose most well-known works are *Go Tell It on the Mountain* and *The Fire Next Time.*

Amiri Baraka (1934-), born Everett LeRoi Jones, is the author of more than forty books of poems, essays, drama, music history, and criticism.

Nikki Giovanni (1943-), born Yolande Cornelia Giovanni, is an American author whose work encompasses poetry, essays, and children's books.

Big Joe Turner (1911-1985) was an African-American blues musician whose 1954 recording, "Shake, Rattle and Roll," was one of the earliest rock and roll songs.

"I have a play called *Big Otis Jump Up Blues Revue*, and it is all about Big Joe Turner jump up blues music. It reminds you of those old race movies. But I decided to see that through a different lens. These are real people, not clowns. These are real people falling in love, falling out of love, working, not working, with great aspirations. They are not clowns with big eyes. I wanted to look at those race movies differently, and as soon as you do that you think, 'Oh, this is something very intense. This has a real life.' You put it in a real-life context."

> Race movies were films produced for African-American audiences that featured all African-American casts. Between 1915 and 1950, approximately 500 race films were produced.

Race Matters

"This African-American sensibility informs my art. This is what I am always reaching for, regardless of what genre I am working in or what type of piece I am working on.

"This is important today," he adds, "because there are a lot of people who think race doesn't matter anymore. In many ways, race *should* not matter. But then you get into the big real world where you are competing for those 'above the line' jobs, jobs that can greenlight a movie and that can make the bigger projects happen, and you realize that race still does matter."

He explains that "above the line" jobs are the positions held by executives and directors in the entertainment industry. "You don't see a lot of Black people in those jobs, and not only Black people but there are very few Hispanics, Asians, and women in positions of power in the entertainment industry.

"Television is still segregated," he adds. "Tell me race doesn't matter when you go watch TV, when you go watch the movies.

"There are very few Black directors who direct white television shows. There are very few music supervisors who are of color. Very few. It is not just Black people that I am talking about here. I am talking about what they call 'minorities,' but I refuse to call us that.

"People of color are not doing the kinds of jobs in the industry where they determine destinies, the kinds of jobs with money and power, the kinds of jobs where you can make a lot of things happen.

"So race does matter. It is changing, absolutely. But when you get above the line where everything happens, you just don't see it."

Sallid reflects on his own successes and adds, "I do know that I have cross a lot of color barriers. I was the first African American to choreograph the Oscars. It had never been done. I have done a lot of those firsts. So sometimes, artistry, telling truths, can overcome barriers."

He explains that when he takes on a director role, he has to arrive not as the "Black" director but as the director. "I must always get rid of it, that race feeling. I can never arrive at the scene with that in my heart. Now that seems like a real contradiction, but if you think about it, my artwork is somewhat complex. It is not binary. It has many things going on that inform where I go—where, why, who.

"Oftentimes I am called upon to do what I will call 'straight white work.' There is nobody of color on the set. There is nobody of color anywhere around me, and the subject matter has nothing to do with anyone of color. Sometimes, I have to inform people of the traditions and of American history. For example, when I was on the show *Suddenly Susan*, they were doing a barbershop quartet. I said, 'You know, that is an African-American art form?' They said, 'Huh?' I had to let them know, and all of sudden they got it and the direction of the piece changed.

"The same thing happened when I worked with Julio Iglesias on his tango album. I said, 'You know that the tango is African, from the slaves in the barrio of Argentina. You've got to have some references on how we got here.' It is so easy to forget. It matters. I have that knowledge, and it informs my work.

Julio Iglesias (1943-) is a Spanish singer and one of the most successful music artists in the world, selling more than 300 million records worldwide.

"It is important to know the history, so that you don't repeat those same kinds of mistakes. But it is more than that," he explains. "You cannot manipulate the language, if you don't understand it. If you don't know the references, you can't really communicate intelligently and you can't be clear about what you want to say.

"Great art is great for a reason. You want to know why. One of the biggest things that artists can do while they are studying is to learn everything."

Listening

Sallid adds this message for aspiring artists: "When I speak to young artists today," he says, "so many of them have a vision that they are this particular thing. They seem to want to get more and more specialized right away."

He mentions a young teacher he recently hired in the charter high school in Van Nuys, California, where he serves as Performing Arts Co-Director. Says Sallid, the young teacher told me that he doesn't like a certain kind of music. I looked at him and I said, "Listen. Really listen."

Sallid recounts his own experiences learning to expand his artistic boundaries. "I was driving down a country road in Arizona, and country music came on the radio. And I said to myself, 'Okay. I get it.' Then I was in Jamaica. I was teaching for the National Dance Theater of Jamaica, and reggae was everywhere. I listened. Really listened. And I suddenly got it.

"For people to say that they don't like a certain kind of music means that they don't get it, they don't understand it. And as an artist, how can you say you don't like a certain kind of music? That says you don't understand it. There is a difference. I think, if you really understand it, you will get it and you will like it.

"If you can speak only one language, you are limiting yourself. You have to able to speak several languages to get it.

"Tell the truth and learn the language. Learn the *languages*," says Sallid. "This is what makes great art."

PART IV

Bringing Joy; Telling the Truth

Introduction

Part IV, Bringing Joy; Telling the Truth, explores the ways that artists bring joy and meaning to the world in which we live. To be an artist involves sharing beauty and happiness. It also means telling the truth, even when that truth is painful. The artists in this section explain their roles in helping to interpret the world.

In Chapter 14, painter and sculptor **Greg Jaris** discusses the role of the regional artist. His approach, he explains, "is to capture the 'here' of my life." He wants his art "to show the magic of the world, the magic of every day." For Jaris, his art "re-enchants the world to its magic."

Ten-time Grammy Award-winner **Bobby McFerrin** explains, in Chapter 15, that "true artists do more than entertain." He continues, "Artistry doesn't just sing. It soars. It lifts people up...[T]he artist gets you to look at yourself in some new way."

In Chapter 16, **Janis Ian** puts it very directly: "Artists tell the truth" and "artists change the world."

The artists in this section stress one of their most important purposes: to help society see, hear, and understand itself—to enable us to translate and make sense of our world.

CHAPTER 14

Greg Jaris

Photo used with permission.

Re-enchanting the World's Magic

Greg Jaris is a painter, a sculptor, a block printer, and a wood-worker. He studied visual arts at Michigan State University, where he earned a Bachelor of Fine Arts in printmaking and drawing, and a Master of Fine Arts in three-dimensional studies and art history. He taught art at Grand Valley State University in Grand Rapids, Michigan, and has worked as a boat builder in Maine and Michigan.

For most of his life, he has made his living as an artist, creating and selling his work in galleries and festivals across the country, especially in Florida and Michigan.

In 1998, Jaris and his wife Linda, also an artist, opened the Trick Dog Gallery in Elberta, Michigan—a tiny village with a population of five hundred, located in northwest lower Michigan, on the Betsie Bay and Lake Michigan. Both a gallery and coffee shop, it has made Elberta a summer destination. Trick Dog's location—overlooking the Bay—and architecture, especially its large and breezy porch, designed by Linda, provides just the right vibe for vacationers, many of whom spend hours sipping cappuccinos and buying art.

In this chapter, Jaris explains that artists capture the "here" of life and help "to show the magic of the world."

Greg Jaris is a multi-faceted visual artist. He paints, sculpts, makes block prints, and works with wood. He is a man of few words, a doer, a creator, and not so much a talker. He emphasizes that everything he does, and everything he has accomplished, is because of his partnership with his wife, Linda. "She has supported everything. We are in this together, raising our daughter together, building our life in art."

The figures in Jaris' work reflect the importance of his family. Much of his art is family self-portraiture. The man depicted is usually an image of Jaris himself—tall, thin, with dark hair. The blonde woman, frequently swimming, is Linda. The child is his daughter Meghan, now grown. And the dogs are the various pets he has had throughout his life—Sadie, Pip, and Trick, the one for whom the gallery is named.

Jaris says that "It is hard for me to describe my art. I don't just paint. I do prints. I do woodworking and ceramics. Some people say this can be detrimental. If you do everything, you never do anything really deeply or as well as someone who specializes. But I don't care. I do what makes sense to me. I will take one idea and try it in all different media. That is what I like to do. I am lucky enough that I can do that."

Some have called his art whimsical, Jaris says, but he doesn't really like that word. "I think it is joyful. Some say it is bizarre, but I don't think my work is bizarre. It is representational with a twist, and that twist goes towards humor."

Jaris wants his art to show the magic of the world, the magic of the everyday. Or as he says: "My art re-enchants the world to its magic.

"But it is simple magic, the magic of life, of living, all those things that we smile at during the day. I try to capture the little things that you do with your dog or your wife or your friends. I try to capture food. Or I try to capture swimming, the feeling of swimming, of being free in the water. The fun stuff, things that make you smile inside."

Jaris describes one of his favorite pieces, *My Dog Likes Sardines*: The six-foot tall wooden cut out of a young man feeding sardines to a large black dog has bright and playful colors. And, despite Jaris' dislike of the word, the image *is* whimsical.

"Now, who would think of this?" asks Jaris. "How do you conceive of an idea like this? I was standing in the kitchen one day, opening a can of sardines. And my beloved Sadie, one of the best dogs I ever had in my life—who isn't with us anymore—just sat there and looked at me. So I took out a fish and gave her one. She just went crazy. She loved it so much.

"In the piece, I wanted to capture the absurdity of this thing—my dog likes to eat fish. That is me. That is how my mind works."

He continues, "I made a piece once of a man holding a frying pan with three fish in it. The piece was called, *Cooking Fish with the Heads On*. That idea came from my daughter, Meghan. When she was little, she once asked, 'What are we having for dinner?' And I said, 'Fish.' And she said, 'Well, you are not going to leave the heads on, are you, Dad?' Because we did that once with trout, and she hated it. And that is a perfect example of an idea for a piece. That is my kind of humor."

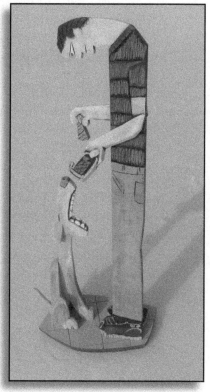

Regional Art

Jaris defines himself as a regional artist. "I depict things, little snippets of regional life. They are not profound ideas. They are things I have done with my daughter or with my wife, things that just happen during the day. I try to write them down or sketch them. I will quickly make a drawing."

Jaris tries to capture the "here" of northern Michigan. "People buy pieces and take them home. The work

My Dog Likes Sardines

reminds them not only of the gallery but of their vacation, the fun time they had, the way that they love this place."

For Jaris, being a regional artist, representing the place where he lives in his art, is important. "The hardest thing for an artist, especially a beginning artist," he says, "is figuring out, 'What should I make? I have skill. What should I do with it?' You have to get in touch with yourself, who you are.

"My approach to ideas is to capture the 'here' of my life. I still don't understand how people can travel to Europe, how they can go to Tuscany and paint and then come back to northern Michigan and have a show about the work they did in Tuscany. That doesn't make sense to me. It is beautiful, but it is so artificial. I would think your mind would get confused about what you are about. You live here. Why not show me *here*, how you think, how you see things?"

Having grown up in a small town, Jaris says that he always wanted to live in a place like Elberta. With a population of five hundred, Elberta is the smallest village in the smallest county, Benzie, in Michigan. He and Linda dreamed of opening their own gallery. It took them a while to reach that dream, but they had a plan and have been successful.

"We thought," says Jaris, "if we make it interesting enough, people will come. We were discouraged, of course. People like to discourage artists all the time. But, your intuition says, 'This has got to work.' We had a different formula, and we approached it as a business."

Jaris believes that every artist needs to remember that an important part of success has less to do with art than it does with business. "Some of it is instinct," he says. "Every artist is unique. You want to exploit your uniqueness somehow. That is the key. You just have to have a gut feeling and go with it with all your energy and another ten percent more. Because it is a lot of hard work—physical, mental, and emotional. Believing in yourself is the thing. If you work hard enough at something, you will persevere."

Even though his gallery is open only in the summer, Jaris works year round creating art, finding merchandise for the store, and deciding what new ideas might be put in place the following summer. "Linda and I work on this all year round," says Jaris. "Summer is kind of relaxing in a way because we can't get anything else done except this store."

Jaris believes that being "in a unique area, a resort area" helps him. "This might not work in a city. But we have new people coming through constantly."

What also helps the business is that Jaris chose a dog focus for his gallery. "It was purely a marketing theme," he explains. "You can't name a gallery a boring or easy-to-forget name. You have to have a zip to your name. And that is the way Trick Dog works—it has that zip. It is a name that prompts curiosity. You say, 'What is that about? It sounds fun. That sounds like something I want to go see.'

"The best galleries work," says Jaris, because they "create a whole world. They create the atmosphere. They become a destination place. You need a name people remember. Think of all the galleries that you have been to, and you can't remember the names."

Trick Dog creates that atmosphere. The guest book includes comment after comment from visitors saying things like, "I LOVE Trick Dog!" "It is a hidden gem on top of a hill in Elberta." "The views are gorgeous, and the quirky, fun artwork makes a great atmosphere both in and out of the cafe." "I love the outdoor seating and browsing the art gallery." "NOT to be missed. Understand? You must go here if you're in the vicinity!"

Influences

Jaris credits his mother with fostering his love of art. "I really think a key part of who I am," he says, "is how I spent my childhood. I had a very good childhood. My parents ran a little mom and pop business. They were always busy.

"This meant that I spent a lot of time alone. I really enjoyed that. I had an older brother, but we weren't that close in age. I lived in a rural community, and I didn't have a lot of playmates. I never felt bad about that, other than that I couldn't play baseball. I love baseball, but there were never enough people for a team.

"I was left alone a lot to my thoughts and to entertain myself. I was, in a way, forced to create my own toys. My mother always encouraged me to make stuff. Even to this day, I find entertainment in really mundane things and enjoy spending time by myself."

Jaris went to Catholic school and was taught by nuns. "I think this has something to do with my self-discipline," he says. "An artist absolutely has to have self-discipline. I am not a religious person now. But this education had a lot to do with who I am.

"I went to college, not knowing what I wanted to do. My mother was constantly telling me, 'You should be an artist,' but I didn't know."

Then, while he was an undeclared student at Michigan State University, Jaris met Linda. "She was an art major, and so I thought, 'Wow, people really do make a living doing this stuff that I have been doing all my life?' It was like a lightning bolt went off. That week, I went to see if I could become an art major."

The university discouraged him. "They said, 'No, no, no. You can't do that. You will have to start from the beginning. You will be a senior in freshmen classes.' But I didn't care if it took forever. I was driven to do this. I had finally found the one thing that I wanted to do.

"This discouragement was the wrong thing to do," Jaris adds. "I would never discourage anyone from following his dream. I always encourage the people who work with me, and any young person I meet, to take as long as you want to get through school. Do not be in a hurry. Just learn."

In college, Jaris met two mentors with whom he maintained a life-long friendship: Lou Raynor and Mel Leiserowitz. Raynor has passed away, and Jaris keeps his portrait in his studio. He still sees Leiserowitz and his wife, Nancy, regularly.

"Raynor," says Jaris, "gave me techniques of working. He gave me mental techniques, not physical techniques. He told me that I could always learn to weld or learn craft. That is not the problem. It is how you approach ideas. He taught me how to look, to see not only art but everything."

> Louis Benjamin Raynor (1917-1999) was a ceramist and professor of art at Michigan State University.

> Mel Leiserowitz (1925-), emeritus professor of art at Michigan State University, is also a sculptor known for his large-scale works in steel.

From Leiserowitz, Jaris believes he has learned "how to balance art and living, and how to enjoy all of life. 'Art creeps in, weaves in, to every-thing,' he would say."

Jaris has taken this lesson literally. He adds art to every aspect of his life. "Like in my kitchen," he says, "if there is a plain wooden handle or something, I just can't stand that. I will take it and carve it in my studio and then put it back in the kitchen. I made a clothesline for my wife, but I couldn't stand having a plain clothesline. Instead, it is two people playing jump rope and holding the line. That is me."

Trust Yourself

Jaris believes he has been very fortunate in his career. "I struggled through like all artists do with no money for a time. But luckily people like my work. I make work for myself, and people *get* it. Sometimes, I make things and I think, 'I am just going to keep this for myself.' Then I will hang it up and someone wants it."

It can still surprise Jaris that people "get" him. This has made him learn to trust himself and his intuition. "This is hard to do," he says, "but it is key. It takes time to learn to trust yourself. They say you need to put in your 10,000 hours as an artist. That's true. You put in your 10,000 hours. You develop your skill and you gain experience. And you have to have the moxie to just keep plugging away.

"This is the only way I think you can do it," says Jaris. "So many art-ists give up before they have really put in their time, either because they are not really driven or they just can't deal with the pressure, the way that artists are not really supported.

"Artists really have to be tough and persevere, because everything in the world is going to be against you. I loved my father, but even after I got my Master of Fine Arts, he said, 'You got your art degree now, that's fine, but what are you going to *do*?' He always thought I should get a teaching degree, too, so I could have something to 'fall back on.' But I always hated the idea of 'falling back.' I was not going to fall."

Jaris remembers that, when he was younger, he would feel some bitterness about the way society treats its artists. "You take a lot of abuse. 'What are you going to do with an art degree?,' they ask. But it is a wonderful background to have. You can enjoy the world in a whole different way and have a whole different view, different from 99 percent of the people. And that is where a liberal arts education comes in, too. Liberal arts study is fantastic. I believe you should study as much of everything as you can. Follow your interests and then you will figure out what you will do."

Jaris also understands that people will change what they do, and change often. This is true not only for artists but for everyone. "If you want to change, change," he says. "Change is good in life. It recharges you. You have to set goals. Set two-, three-, and four-year goals.

"For me, I wanted to build a studio, and then I wanted to pay for that studio within a certain amount of time. Well, that drove me to work. I knew that to have that studio, I needed to get it paid off. These goals helped to keep me focused. Do not be afraid of your goals or your interest in changing."

Jaris' career took him down several roads. After graduate school, he and Linda opened a ceramics studio. Ceramics, says Jaris, "is one of the easiest way to make some money as an artist. We started selling our work on the street, before art fairs are what they are now. We were selling work in galleries. Anyplace we could, we sold our work."

Jaris then took a full-time teaching position at Grand Valley State University, in Grand Rapids, Michigan, where he taught ceramics, drawing, and design. He recalls, "I taught for five or six years, and then the economy went bad in Michigan, and I got laid off. Almost the whole art department did. I had to decide again what to do. I really didn't like university teaching, because the university wouldn't let me teach. They would find just a zillion other things for me to do, like recruiting. Yet, I thought I was an excellent teacher.

"When I was laid off, I got disgusted with art for a while. I sold everything in my studio. My mentors were mad, but they knew that this can happen, that artists can get discouraged and that they will come back to it. They had faith in me, which was fortunate. I could always talk with them. I could say that I was fed up, and they would listen. They would just let me figure it out.

"So I decided to teach myself another craft."

Jaris went to Maine to learn boat building. He brought this craft back with him to Michigan, where he built small row boats from cedar. He says, "For me, even though the boat building thing was a diversion from art, it really improved my woodworking skills. If you can build a boat out of wood, you can build anything out of wood.

"I find this exciting as an artist. I have the skills to make whatever I can think of out of wood. No matter how absurd it is, I can make it. And that is really a neat thing. That is a great place to be in your career. You don't have to worry. The skill level is not in the way. Craft is not a problem. And that is a goal to strive for, because then the making of art becomes second nature, like signing your name. You do not have to think about how to do something and can concentrate on making what you want to make."

Jaris started making furniture and decided he liked that better than boat building. There was less pressure and fewer regulations. And it was more profitable than boat making.

He entered the Coconut Grove Arts Festival in Miami, at that time a very prestigious art festival. "I put my things on the street and sold everything on the first day. I thought, 'I am back in the art business.'" While in Miami, he picked up gallery connections. He returned to Michigan and made furniture that was painted with bold colors and sometimes elaborate designs. Soon, he stopped making furniture and just concentrated on the painting. Recalls Jaris, "I went to my old teachers and said, 'I'm painting.' And they said, 'Good, good.' They were always encouraging me to do anything. They said, 'Just paint.' And I did."

Driven to Create

Jaris is incredibly prolific. "I am obsessive almost," he laughs. "But age is slowing me down. I used to work late at night, but I don't any more. I work in the morning."

Jaris adds, "The way I work, I always have sixteen things I want to do ahead of me, because this one piece makes me want to create these other pieces, which will be better than this piece.

"That is the cliché, isn't it," he asks, "that the next piece will be my best? That is what keeps me driven. I like to work."

Jaris sketches every day, jotting down all the ideas that come to him. He reviews those sketches and pulls out ideas when their time has come. He explains, "For any visual artist, drawing is one of the most important things. You can't be a good visual artist without good drawing skills. That is absolutely necessary. You need to be able to translate your thoughts onto a piece of paper. For me, it is like putting my mind on the page. I am able to take this abstract thing that is kind of floating out there and make it concrete, make it real. I don't have to draw finished drawings. I just draw."

Having his own gallery and control over his work means that Jaris is able to focus on what he most enjoys. "As an artist, I found that one of the most difficult things was repeating myself. Galleries want you to repeat yourself. If they sell something, they want you to come back with more of the same. That is one of the main reasons that drove me to have my own gallery, so that I can do what I want. I never have to repeat work, unless I want to. I don't repeat myself now. I do series of things."

He explains that he creates what he loves. "I like bold and quick images. I paint quickly. I need images to appear quickly, or I move on. I pick techniques that allow me to get images quickly. That is why I don't carve. To sit and carve a person or a dog out of wood would bore me to death. I want the image as quickly as I can get it. And that is why the images evolve as they do. They are simple. They are two-dimensional. They are planes. I like the idea of putting planes together and making a three-dimensional object with two-dimensional planes."

Whimsy in History

In addition to his drive to create, Jaris loves to read history and archeology. He is fascinated by the photos in archeology magazines. "When I look at them," he says, "I notice the background more than the foreground. I am fascinated by what the photo is not about. I just *love* what they are *not* telling me."

Having recently traveled to Europe, Jaris has rekindled a fascination with Gothic works. "I love the Gothic stare," he says. "I find the sculptures on all these buildings in Europe very funny. There is a whimsical element to them. I am sure that is what the artists had in mind when they created them. They were trying to be funny.

"I like the little twist in art. I like to put that in my own work, to keep people off guard, to make them question what I am doing. I am sure that is what those medieval artists wanted to do. I am mischievous, visually mischievous, and that is how I see those Gothic pieces.

"I love Etruscan art, too," he continues. "Etruscan people are real funny people. They had an attitude towards life that was totally different from the Romans. If you look at Etruscan art, you will see that their work is like what I try to do in art. For instance, the figures that they sculpted will have a smirk on them, and you know it is not a mistake smirk. That makes the artist human for me. This shows that the sculpture was not just some obscure thing, but that it was made by someone on purpose, and that person had a particular idea that he wanted to share. A person who I can relate to made it. I enjoy that."

Jaris "enjoys art in a different way than most people. I imagine the artist. We have this idea from history that there were people pounding out this work as if it were just a job and not something that was personal or meant something to them. But they were real people. They had lunch, and they had a headache, and they had an argument with their wife. You can see that this work has a human quality. It is not just an image anymore."

Making Art Accessible

Just as the artists come to life for Jaris, he tries to make his art come to life for the people who enter his gallery. "I don't want people to be intimidated by my art or my gallery," he says. "I don't like that. I still get intimidated going to art galleries sometimes. Some of them are obnoxiously formal. And I am an artist.

"I believe everyone should fill their life with color and fun. I want to create unique pieces that will make you smile and laugh. And I want to offer some things for just a little money, so that people are not afraid to make that first investment."

Jaris explains that he prices some of his prints very inexpensively. If people buy that first piece cheaply, if they enjoy it, he says, they will come back and buy something else, maybe spending a little more the next time.

Art should be for everyone, he states. "I don't believe in the preciousness of art. Art should be enjoyed," says Jaris, "and when works of art wear out, they wear out, like we all do. I enjoy looking at all the old pieces of art, in Europe and elsewhere. Most of them will last a really long time, longer than maybe they should even, but once they have died, let them die. That is okay. Document them now, but let them die."

Jaris explains that he destroys a lot of his own work. "You know," he says, "when prints are misprinted and they are not quite done right, well, maybe I could give them away or sell them for a discount, like some artists do, but I just tear them up and throw them away. That doesn't bother me.

"We hold too much art as precious. You know, that money and effort and life energy could be better spent doing something else, something towards living. We can make something new, something that people can enjoy, that can make people smile. That is what art is about, at least for me."

My Dog Smiles When I Come Home

CHAPTER 15

Bobby Mcferrin

Photo used with permission.

Spreading Joy

A ten-time Grammy-Award winner, Bobby McFerrin is a vocal innovator and improviser. He is an eternal seeker, always pushing the boundaries beyond traditional definitions. The creator of the hit work "Don't Worry, Be Happy," his recordings have sold over twenty million copies, and his collaborations include those with Yo-Yo Ma, Chick Corea, and Herbie Hancock.

With his four-octave range and his vast array of vocal techniques, McFerrin is a musical explorer who combines jazz, folk, and world music influences—choral, a cappella, and classical music—with his unique style. As a conductor, he has worked with, among others, the New York Philharmonic, the Cleveland Orchestra, the Chicago Symphony, the Philadelphia Orchestra, and the Vienna Philharmonic.

McFerrin's career can best be described as unconventional. Each performance is unique and resonates with the unexpected. As an artist, he is able to reach beyond musical genres and stereotypes for a sound that is entirely his own. McFerrin's music is natural, timeless, transcends all borders, and embraces all cultures.

In the following pages, McFerrin explains that "True artists do more than entertain." They help us look at ourselves "in some new way."

Vocalist, improviser, and conductor Bobby McFerrin has just one goal when he performs: "to bring joy to people. That is what it is all about for me. And I get joy when I invite the audience on stage with me to sing or to dance."

Performing solo concerts for nearly thirty years, McFerrin has invited the audience on stage for at least the last fifteen. He explains, "I like to invite twenty singers on stage to make a choir for the night, to improvise with them. There are so many wonderful artists out there. I invite anyone who wants to join me."

He laughs, "A lot of people don't believe it at first. They don't believe that I am asking for people to come up. Someone always asks if those were plants. Was that really all improvised, or had I planned it out? They can't believe that I am that spontaneous in inviting anyone who wants to join me to do just that.

"Sometimes you get some really extraordinary voices, just fantastic. And then," he laughs again, "you get the singers who shouldn't be singing at all. But I do my best to create something that they can sing, so that it is gratifying for everyone. I try to meet them where they are.

"That is always joyful for me. I get satisfaction from the great singers and from the ones that aren't so great. At least people see that they had the courage to attempt something.

"Then," says McFerrin, "at the end of the concert, instead of doing an encore, I usually open it up to questions and answers. I have the house lights turned on and I ask people if they would like to get to know me a little better. I am just a regular person. I am an audience member from time to time myself. So I just like to relax and have a good time."

McFerrin explains that since he started giving solo performances, his hope has been "to knock down the wall between the performer and the audience. That was always my goal. If I wasn't inviting individuals on stage, I invited the audience to sing. I don't think it has ever happened during a concert of mine that the audience hasn't participated in one form or another. From the very beginning, I always wanted to engage the audience in such a way that they actively participated in the performance.

"Audiences are different. They have a cultural personality. Sometimes, depending on the country that I am in, it takes a lot of coaxing to get them to sing along with me. Then, in other cultures, I just point and they are ready to go. By now, people have come to expect that they are going to sing with me. Some of them even buy their tickets early, so that they can get good seats and are close enough, so they can get to the stage quickly to sing with me. I enjoy that.

"I was calling it audience art for a while."

Changing People's Hearts

McFerrin believes strongly that "True artists do more than entertain. They have a positive effect on you. I will never forget, one time after a performance, I had opened it up for questions and answers at the end, and this woman stood up and she said, 'I don't know about anybody else here, but I feel so much better now. You made me feel so good.'

"To me, that is absolutely what it is all about. I made her feel good. She made me feel good. We all felt good. That is the bottom line."

"Artistry does that," continues McFerrin. "It doesn't just sing. It soars. It lifts people up. It not only gets you to tap your feet and move your body. Through the music, the artist gets you to look at yourself in some new way. It is not about looking at the artist so much but about looking at whatever the artist is showing you that relates to you—your own personality, your own being—that makes you think about your life and what you're doing. It is not just, 'Wow, man, you're really cool. I really like what you do,' but it is, 'I really like what you have done for me or what you do to me.'

"Artists," says McFerrin, "should be in the business of heart surgery, changing people's hearts."

McFerrin recalls the artists who changed his heart and helped to shape him. "When I saw Miles Davis for the first time, the band was just so unbelievable that I literally was changed. I felt that my entire molecular structure went through a complete overhaul. Even physically, my body felt different. I remember walking out of that place completely stunned.

"What they were showing me was how engaging and wonderful and challenging improvisation was. Even though I knew what improvisation was, in theory, I had never really experienced it like that. I had never heard a group play together that way, listen to one another that way, and reflect one another in that way. That was a pivotal moment for me.

"That is what we should be doing as artists—changing a person's atmosphere. That is the real meaning of a true artist. Artists do that. They have that effect on people. At the end of it, all of a sudden, time has been transcended. You have been sitting in this seat for two hours, and it felt like two minutes, and you just want it to go on and on and on."

McFerrin hopes to create a space where those who come to hear him are transcended. He also seeks to engage others, especially those he invites on stage, in the joy of improvisation, a form of art he believes helps to change people in a deep way.

He explains, "Anyone can improvise, if they understand that improvisation is motion. You don't have to necessarily know anything intellectually or theoretically to do it. Anyone can continue to play notes on the piano or play notes on their horn or sing note after note after note. That is all they have to do.

"Obviously, the more you know theoretically, the more you know about music, the more information that you can use when you are improvising. But motion is first and then knowledge. Most people thought that knowledge was first and then motion, but it's not. It's the other way around.

"When I saw Miles play, that came to me, even though I couldn't have defined it at the time. I went for weeks and weeks not really understanding what I heard. All I knew is how I felt at the end of it. I thought that something had been revealed to me that I hadn't known before, something very exciting, even though I didn't understand it. They just kept pushing each other to keep going, go higher, go further, go deeper, just keep moving. That is what improvisation is. Anybody can do that."

Growing Up in a House of Music

Breaking down the separation between performer and audience comes naturally to McFerrin. He was born into music and grew up believing that his art was a natural part of who he was. He wants everyone to see music as an organic part of life, connected to—not separate from—the everyday.

"I grew up in a house of music," he explains. "I started studying piano in Julliard's preparatory department music training when I was six years old. I was on the piano everyday. I did not think of myself as a musician, really. It was just something that I did. It was like playing ball or playing games with friends."

McFerrin's late father, Robert McFerrin, Sr., an operatic baritone, was the first African-American male soloist at the Metropolitan Opera. His mother, singer Sara Copper, is a former soloist with regional companies and is professor emeritus of music at Fullerton College. "There was music everywhere," says McFerrin.

He remembers his decision to study music in college as a casual one. "When I was a senior in high school," he recalls, "the guidance counselor called me in one day. He asked me what I was planning to do when I went to college. What were my goals? We had that kind of conversation. I remember saying something really casual, like, 'Well, I guess I'll be a musician,' because it wasn't something I struggled with. It was so natural. It wasn't something I thought about: 'What am I going to do when I grow up?' I just assumed it would be in music."

Knowing Oneself through Moments

McFerrin recalls important moments in his life, moments that helped to shape and define him. "My life has sort of been dotted with moments that have kept me going," he explains.

McFerrin studied piano and composition at the University of California, Santa Cruz. "That is what I was interested in," says McFerrin, "composing, particularly for films and for television, the Hollywood composing scene."

Dave Grusin (1934-) is a Grammy and Oscar-winning composer and arranger who has scored such films as *The Firm* and *The Milagro Beanfield War*.

He recalls an important mentor, one he met while he was in college—Dave Grusin. "Grusin was an idol for me. At that time, he wrote for a lot of TV shows. His name was on a lot of albums. He scored for a lot of movies. I found his name in the musicians' union book and called him. Someone answered and told me that he was working on a film at Paramount Studios. They took my name and number. That surprised me. Then, three days later, Grusin actually called me back and invited me to his studio.

"He told me to bring my compositions, so he could take a look at them. He invited me to a scoring session. He was working on a film with Robert Redford, and he introduced me to all the musicians playing in the band.

"It was amazing that he did this for me. That was one of those moments that kept my musical fires going. To this day, I am grateful. We have become friends. We've worked together and have hung out. He likes to tell people that he has known me since I was nineteen. That was one of those moments that kept me going."

McFerrin sees another life-defining moment when he decided to be a singer. "I had sung before. I had sung in bands and background parts. Or I would take a lead vocal on a song occasionally, but I never thought of myself as a singer.

"One day, I was living in Salt Lake City and I was accompanying a dance class on the piano. I was walking home for lunch. Somewhere between my dance class and walking home, I suddenly realized, 'I'm a singer.' There wasn't any thunder or lightning or anything like that. It was just this *knowing* that singing was probably my instrument.

"And," says McFerrin, "I got a job the very next day, singing and playing at a piano bar at a hotel in Salt Lake."

He points to another moment, later in his career, when he had branched out as a conductor. "There was a time after conducting for about three years, I thought about giving it up. I was really discouraged because I wasn't getting any kind of respect. People saw me as the 'Don't Worry, Be Happy' guy, who didn't really know much of anything outside of pop or jazz, so I was having difficulty with some orchestras. I was just about to take the baton and break it over my knee.

"I was in Hamburg, Germany. I was about to do a performance with an orchestra that had been giving me a rough time all week long. I thought, 'I'm not going to do this.'

"Prior to that, I had been exploring different conductors and watching different conductors, getting films on conductors and the art of conducting. And I discovered a conductor by the name of Carlos Kleiber. There are great, great conductors, but I thought Kleiber was the most extraordinary conductor I had ever seen. Profound, simply profound. I had never experienced anything like him.

"I was backstage pacing, having this very negative conversation with myself thinking, 'I don't want to do this. I am going to tell my agent after this

Carlos Kleiber (1930-2004) was an Austrian classical conductor considered by many to be the greatest conductor of his generation.

that I am not conducting anymore.' When, lo and behold, twenty minutes before I was to go on, I got a note from Carlos Kleiber." He laughs. "The note said, 'Good luck on your new endeavors,' signed, 'A fan, Carlos Kleiber.' I didn't even know that he knew I existed, and here I get a note from him claiming that he is a fan, and he is wishing me the best of luck.

"Well, we proceeded to have some correspondence, writing letters to each other. He wrote me this wonderful two-page letter on conducting. So here is another moment, a critical moment, when I am thinking about making some changes, when I get some encouragement from this wonderful man."

McFerrin also recalls an important moment with tenor Plácido Domingo in Paris in 2008. "I had met Plácido Domingo prior to that. Before my performance, he came backstage to let me know that he was there and that he could stay only for thirty minutes, because he had a rehearsal to go to. I thought, 'This is great. Plácido Domingo came to see me.' So, after singing for about twenty-five minutes, I took a chance and from the stage asked if Plácido Domingo was still in the house. And he said that he was. I had them turn on the house lights. He was sitting in the first balcony in the center.

Plácido Domingo (1941-), a Spanish tenor and conductor, is known primarily for his opera roles and as one of The Three Tenors.

"I asked him if he knew the Bach-Gounod Ave Maria, and he said that he did. I asked him if he would be willing to sing it. He wasn't sure if he wanted to, but we coaxed him into doing it. People at the orchestra level had turned around and were facing the balcony. Anyway, I sang the Bach and he sang the Gounod, and it was one of the most thrilling moments of my life.

"As it turned out, he stayed for the rest of the performance. I don't know what happened to the rehearsal. But he stayed. My wife was sitting up in the row with him, and she said that, by the end, he was so excited, just like a little boy who had gotten a new toy. He was very excited about it. That was a very special moment for me."

Fame and Faith

McFerrin has had a great deal of success in his life. With that success has come fame. "Fame wasn't something that I sought," he says. "In the beginning, it was very uncomfortable for me, because I was always a guarded and private person, and all of a sudden people were peeking into my life and stepping into my space, and I didn't like it.

"On one hand," he says, "I was flattered. Who wouldn't be? On the other hand, I found it very disruptive. So, Deb, my wife, and I, had to figure out a way to preserve some normalcy in our lives, because all of a sudden I was in the spotlight. We were invited to some extraordinary events, which was very wonderful. We've been to the White House a few times. That's cool. But it was very, very different from what we were used to. We had to make some adjustments. That took a long time. Now, the fame is almost normal, because I have gotten used to it."

McFerrin reiterates that fame was not anything he sought. "It just happened, because I sang well and I worked hard. I was working as a musician, and that's what I wanted to do. All my life, my goal was to be able to make my living in music. Then, all of a sudden, one morning I woke up and discovered that I had an album that sold ten million copies."

McFerrin's 1988 release "Don't Worry, Be Happy" became the first a cappella song to reach number one on *Billboard* magazine's Hot 100 chart, and held that position for two weeks. In 1989, it also won Grammys for Song of the Year and Record of the Year. In addition, McFerrin won the Grammy for Best Pop Vocal Performance, Male.

Everything changed as a result of this, says McFerrin. "All of a sudden, I'm on these TV shows." But for McFerrin, it also was, at times, overwhelming.

He continues, "Young people shouldn't seek fame. That shouldn't be why they do what they do. That is a lousy reason for being an artist. If young people are thinking about going into the business, because they want to be famous, it will be harder for them. If you become desperate because you want to be famous, then you will end up doing anything. Some young kids fall into this. They think being the bad boy or the bad girl is where it's at, because you get a lot of notoriety and a lot of attention."

McFerrin explains the ways he tries "to catch" himself when he feels being changed by fame. "I try to watch myself when my ego starts to take off or I feel like I am showing off, when I am tempted to be something, to be somebody.

"It is very difficult to maintain personal integrity," he says. "But I work at it. I recognize that I have this gift and I have this talent and I can do what I do, and it is a constant battle not to show off, not to be anything other than just my regular self. I got caught in this trap early on, too. People pay money to hear you and to look at you.

"It can really kind of inflate you, and you can lose your sense of self. And I can attest to that, because it happened to me. I got intoxicated with applause and approval. It is very intoxicating. I wonder how these young kids who make it at sixteen, seventeen, eighteen, nineteen, twenty years old, how they handle it.

"By the time I started to get some celebrity status," he says, "I was in my mid-thirties and I even had a hard time with it, because it was just so unusual and different."

To maintain balance and a sense of himself, McFerrin, a man of faith, makes sure that he prays every day. "I pray a lot," he says. "I fall back on my faith often throughout the day. I read the Bible often. I watch what I eat. I try to drink plenty of water and get lots of rest. I remind myself that I am not here to entertain as much as I am to attain some inner emotional balance with myself and with the audience."

"I am trying to cool hot hearts, to soothe troubled hearts. I think that music is a great tool for that, for emotional healing, balancing a person out. But I have to struggle with it. I have to keep reminding myself of that, because I am on stage singing, and I will do something, and you can hear some people go, 'Oh, wow. How did he do that?' and all that kind of stuff. And that can make you think, 'Wow, this is pretty cool.'

"But as soon as I do, I try to remind myself, 'Wait now, hold on now, back up here.'

"Anybody who has some kind of fame will tell you that if you are trying to practice your faith and maintain some kind of integrity or at least humbly submit to the fact that you have been given a gift and to be grateful for it, it can be a struggle to be regular or, as the Amish say, 'to be plain.'"

McFerrin continues, "I have always tried to be humble and faithful. Now I do this so often, work on my humility, that I have to think less about it than I used to."

When touring, maintaining his sense of balance can be even more difficult. "Being on the road, it really weighs you down," says McFerrin. "It is hard to tour. Different hotels just about every night. Two or three flights to get to where you need to get to. On touring days, I get to my hotel, I have time for a meal. Then I have to do a sound check. Maybe I have a press conference and interviews. Then there is time for a quick dinner. Then I do the show.

"I avoid receptions. I avoid parties. After the gig, get me back to my hotel room, so I can take a nice soothing bath and read a book and get some sleep. Because I have to get up and do the same thing the next day. I really try to take care of myself, because touring is very strenuous."

He adds, "The only thing I don't like about touring is touring. I love the gig, but I hate the time it takes to get there. I am looking forward to those days when they develop those transporting machines, like in *Star Trek*, and you can just show up at the gig, beam yourself onto the stage, and beam yourself home afterwards."

Finding Balance

For McFerrin, figuring out ways to balance his time with family and his career has been an important achievement. It is the accomplishment of which he is most proud.

McFerrin and his wife, Deb, have been married for over thirty-five years. "All three of my kids really like me. They want to spend time with me, and I cannot wait to spend time with them. They are the joy of my heart," he says. "I am just grateful that I have such a wonderful, wonderful family. That means more to me than anything else in this world."

He worked hard to keep his family a priority.

He explains that from 2001 to 2005 or so, "I was on the road just at this horrendous pace. We had just moved from Minnesota to Philadelphia, and I had mortgages and expenses up the yin yang. And I basically had to just stay out on the road."

But he didn't like it and wanted to change it. He worked with his manager to put in place what he has now achieved: He tours for six months of every year and is home for six months.

It took five years to accomplish this goal, he explains. He started with an eighteen-month sabbatical. "I was exhausted," he says, "and needed a break. When I came out of the sabbatical, I did eight months on and four months off. I couldn't get to six months on and six months off right away. It took me a long time to get to that point, five years. But my business manager knew it was important to me and worked on it for me."

Personal and professional commitments are important to McFerrin, key to the balance he has created for himself. He says, "I have had the same manager for more than thirty years, the same road manager for more than twenty years, and the same business manager for over twenty-five years. When you find the right people to work with, you want to make that work."

These long relationships are, says McFerrin, "very balancing. They are real. We know each other. We understand one another. How many managers who, when 'Don't Worry, Be Happy' came out, would say, 'Okay, go take the sabbatical that you had planned to take'? 'Don't Worry, Be Happy' just started flying out the stores, and it was selling gobs and gobs. All these opportunities were coming. I was getting invitations to be in films, to open up the Grammys, to appear on the Academy Awards. What manager would have stuck by my decision to stay on a sabbatical when my song was doing so well? Most would say, 'Let's milk this. Let's do the "Don't Worry, Be Happy" tour. Let's do all the television appearances. Now is your time. This is what we've been working for all these years.'

"But my manager was totally fine with my taking a sabbatical. Because she knew I was physically tired. She knew I wouldn't be able to do it. I'd burn out. She knew how important it was for me to reconnect with my family, to be home for a while.

"So she was able to see beyond the immediate gratification to long term goals of just simply working. Now that's wonderful management. That's a real relationship. So I'm committed to her. She's committed to me. And it just makes for longevity, when you are in relationships that are meaningful and deeply rooted in something beyond yourself. I really value commitment a lot."

McFerrin is grateful that he has achieved his goal—living his life as a working musician.

He is grateful that he has been able to "keep it real," to build a strong family, and to be grounded. And, he is so very grateful that he has been able to make the world a little better by bringing joy to people through music.

CHAPTER 16

Janis Ian

Photo used with permission.

Being an Artist

Janis Ian is a singer, songwriter, columnist, and author. She began her career in the 1960s and has continued recording and touring ever since, with a discography of twenty-five albums, including her two-CD set, Best of Janis Ian: The Autobiography Collection. *She now runs her own record label, Rude Girl Records.*

A child prodigy, at the age of twelve in 1963, she wrote her first song, "Hair of Spun Gold." In 1967, at sixteen, her song "Society's Child (Baby I've Been Thinking)," about an interracial romance forbidden by a girl's mother, became a national hit. The album that featured "Society's Child," Janis Ian, *was nominated for a Grammy for Best Folk Performance in 1967. And in 2001, "Society's Child" was inducted into the Grammy Hall of Fame.*

Ian's most successful single in the United States, "At Seventeen," was released in 1975 and reached number three on the Billboard *magazine charts. The song's album,* Between the Lines, *also hit number one on* Billboard's *album chart. That year, Ian received four Grammy nominations, including Song of the Year, Record of the Year, and Album of the Year. She won two Grammys that year: Best Female Pop Vocals—At Seventeen, and Best Engineered Recording—Between the Lines.*

Many other artists have recorded Ian's songs, most notably Roberta Flack, who had a hit in 1974 with "Jesse," Joan Baez, Dottie West, Cher, Puff Daddy, Mel Tormé, Amy Grant, Sheena Easton, and Bette Midler.

Ian was one of the first artists to release her songs for free download on the Internet and was one of the first to show evidence that free downloads increase hard-copy sales. Her 2002 article on this subject, "The Internet Debacle: An Alternate View," written for Performing Songwriter, *has become a classic text.*

Ian has been a regular columnist for, and still contributes to, the gay rights news magazine, The Advocate. *She also contributed a column to* Performing Songwriter *magazine from 1995 through 2003.*

In addition, Ian writes science fiction. In 2003, she co-edited, with Mike Resnick, the anthology Stars: Original Stories Based on the Songs of Janis Ian.

In 2008, Ian released her autobiography Society's Child.

In this chapter, Ian explains why the world needs artists: Artists tell the truth and artists change the world.

Janis Ian defines herself "as an artist. I let it go at that," she says. For Ian, being an artist means that "the rest is not relevant. It doesn't matter that I am Jewish. It does not matter that I am female. All those things inform my work and inform my life, but those are accidents of birth.

"Talent is also an accident of birth," she says. "To become an artist takes a lot more than talent. To become an artist is a long, slow, arduous process. Artists are committed to their art above all else. Being an artist, creating art, takes time, passion, and dedication. It is also about focus to one's art; it takes courage."

Ian adds, "Artists tell the truth"—even if that truth is painful to tell and painful to hear, even if the truth is unpopular, questions the status quo, or challenges authority. "Artists change the world," she says. "They hold chaos at bay. Artists are storytellers. Artists keep our history for us. And artists are different from people who are famous."

Art versus Fame

Being an artist is not about being famous, says Ian. This important theme for her is something that she learned over time. "My sense of myself has changed with age. When I was much younger, my goal was to be famous. Then my goal was to be a good artist and a good writer. Then my goal was to make enough money that I could stay home. Now it is just to get through the rest of my life with some dignity and some joy."

Ian emphasizes the distinction between being famous and being an artist. "In America," says Ian, "it is good to be famous. It is considered a valid thing to have as a life goal.

"But," she continues, "I think there is a real danger in this, when an entire society thinks that being famous isn't weird. When I was a kid, you had only seven television channels in New York City and no music magazines other than *Downbeat* and *Broadside* and a couple of 'teen scream'-type magazines. If you wanted to be famous, people thought there was something weird about you. I think that is rather healthy. Being famous should not be a life goal.

"Certainly, being famous does not make you a better musician. It does not make you a better writer. It doesn't make you anything except maybe a bit of money and maybe some notoriety. Timothy McVeigh is as famous as you can get in America. Who wants that? The line between famous and notorious has really become so blurred. It can be very confusing, especially to young people.

Timothy McVeigh was responsible for the 1995 bombing of an Oklahoma City federal building, which killed 168 people. He was executed in 2001.

"Today, there are just so many magazines, so many TV stations, the Internet—there is so much exposure that fame really changes people and it is, ultimately, very destructive to the society." Popular media focus on what is not important—a star's drug habits or excesses, rather than on the seriousness of art.

"There was a point in my life when I really wanted to be a Beatle, or at least as famous as The Beatles were. That was the most important thing. I had enough sense to learn that writing hit songs was really a better road for me, because I had also been raised to want to be what I was, which I thought was a writer of songs that had some meaning."

Something inside of You

Ian studied with Stella Adler, the American actor and acclaimed acting teacher who founded the Stella Adler Studio of Acting in New York City. Ian credits Adler with helping her understand some of the most important aspects of being an artist.

Says Ian, "Stella Adler once said to my class that we thought we were doing this—acting, singing, studying—because we wanted to be famous, but in fact we were doing this, because there was something inside of us too big to get out any other way.

"I think that is a really valid description," says Ian. "It is one of the reasons why I tell art students and young artists today that no one else in the world has the same vision as you do, and whether you are a writer or a singer or a player, whatever you are in the arts, you have a right to your vision. I should say that whether you are in the arts or not, you have the absolute right to your vision. Hold on to it and to enjoy it.

Ian recalls different choices she has made in her life, times when she put her creativity and artistry on hold in order to satisfy the demands of fame. "I remember a time, when I was twenty or maybe twenty-four, I was sitting on the stoop with my ex-boyfriend, Peter, and I told him that I was going on tour for the next ten months. He said it would destroy my writing for that time period. I said, 'You are absolutely right. It will harshly affect my writing, but I would like to make enough money, so that I can then be a writer forever.' It did not work out that way, so apparently that was not in the master plan. But it was good for me to experience fame.

"Famous has so many options and so many different degrees. Right now, I am what I call semi-famous. This is really the way that I like to refer to it. To me, semi-famous gives me the luxury of making a living doing music and writing. I don't have to have a day job outside of my music, but I do have a day job, in a way. My day job is being 'Janis Ian' and doing the business of Janis Ian."

For Ian, a star since she was a teen, putting on the persona of Janis Ian is work. Managing her record company and web site is work. Doing the touring that she does is work. But all of it is tied to her life choice as an artist.

Being Real and Letting Your Ego Go

Ian emphasizes the importance of artists being true to themselves. "There is a way to be a performer that is not fake, that is true to what you are," she says. She explains that being true to yourself is not the same as revealing yourself, your intimate details, on or off stage.

She explains, "By 'being real,' I don't mean getting up on stage and being yourself. That is not it at all." The audience does not really care about who you are as an individual. Says Ian, "As a member of the audience, I want to be blown away. I want to be moved and astounded and astonished. I want to feel like that was the greatest thing that I have seen in decades."

Performers, Ian continues, take the "best parts of themselves and the parts that work on stage, and make those parts more and more comfortable on stage, more and more confident. When I am Janis Ian on stage, I am not Janis with a cold or a headache or grumpy Janis. Who cares about that? I am Janis Ian, singer-songwriter. Because, once you find something that works, you stick with it. I believe that we all know a lot of this already. Performers know the best parts of themselves in their core.

"Art is, in part, the stripping away of everything else until you have the core talent. I think that a lot of people probably believe that talent is enough. But it is not. It is not nearly enough. It is way too competitive, if you want to make a living.

"In the performing arts, you need a lot of ego to get on stage and assume that, not only will people stay, but they will come back at intermission, and they won't throw things, and they won't talk while you are up there."

Ian discusses how challenging it can be to balance the ego needed to be an artist with the insecurities that come from choosing a path that is really considered so socially unacceptable. She explains, "No matter how much society thinks being famous is cool, it is also telling you, 'What do you mean you are going to be a musician? That is no way to earn a living. Go do something else.' My Mom made me learn typing."

Art Is Universal

"Art," says Ian, "is universal. Art is not concerned with you. I would argue that we don't care what Beethoven was like as a person. We don't care what he was like in bed. We care about his music.

"In writing my autobiography," says Ian, "I had really to remember what it is like to be eighteen or twenty and just starting out. You are so sure that everyone is looking at you. You are so awkward. It is so hard.

"I hope that young people can learn from my mistakes," she continues, "because I sure made a lot of them." She laughs. "But I do know that, as artists, we need to reinvent the wheel all the time, because that is how we are built. As an artist, you have to accept responsibility for your decisions, and you have to insist on the ability to make your decisions, even if you will make mistakes."

Continues Ian, "Performers at a young age—at eighteen, twenty, twenty-two, even twenty-five, thirty—I think you have the ego that a baby has, sort of, 'Look at me, look at me. Aren't I fabulous? Aren't I wonderful?' I was just like this. I am not saying anything that I did not experience.

"When I hit my forties, I realized that I will never be the youngest again, I will never be thought amazing again, because everyone expects that of me. Once I got to picking myself up off the floor, I realized my life is not nearly as interesting as what I can write about.

"At the risk of being rude, I have very little patience for the school of songwriting that focuses on 'I feel this, I feel that.' I have very little patience

> Thelonious Monk (1917-1982) was an American pianist who helped develop bebop music and is one of the most recorded jazz composers of all time.

for that, because it is just not that interesting, unless you hit a universal. Art, in large part, is a search for the universal. It is impossible to conduct this search if all you care about is yourself. Whether it is Miles Davis or Thelonious Monk or Janis Ian or Bob Dylan, it is a search to hit that universal moment with a piece that cuts through all the bullshit and goes straight to the heart. That is art."

Berklee College of Music Keynote Address

What follows is Janis Ian's keynote address, given at Berklee College of Music's Liberal Arts Symposium, April 9, 2010. Ian was the first recipient of the Berklee Liberal Arts Tribute Award, an annual award given to an artist who demonstrates outstanding achievement in artistry and education. The Liberal Arts Symposium is an annual college-wide address given by an artist or scholar, who emphasizes the importance of having a broad worldview and understanding the relationship between art and society. Ian gave this address after spending a week on Berklee's campus, interacting with students and faculty. This address clearly presents Janis Ian's understanding of artistry and offers important lessons for all of us.

Pat Pattison is a Professor at Berklee College of Music, where he teaches Lyric Writing and Poetry. He is the author of three books, *Writing Better Lyrics*, *Songwriting: Essential Guide to Lyric Form and Structure*, and *Songwriting: Essential Guide to Rhyming*.

I have to confess that when Pat Pattison began asking me to do a Berklee residency about fifteen years ago, my reaction was complete disbelief. I left school in tenth grade. The very day I turned sixteen, I left, walked out the door, and never looked back. I have never regretted that decision. I was not made to be in a school. I do not play well with others. When I run with scissors, it's usually with the intention of sticking them into someone's back....

But Pat is nothing if not persistent, and so, here I am.

Friedrich Nietzsche (1844-1900) was a German philosopher whose most famous works include *Thus Spoke Zarathustra* and *Beyond Good and Evil*.

Once I'd accepted President Roger Brown's and Pat's kind invitation, and they mentioned that there was a keynote speech involved, I thought I would do the standard keynote. I would congratulate everyone on leaving school eventually and entering the wide world of the music business. I would offer some cautionary tales and have done with it. But... the more I thought about that, the more I realized I really had nothing to say about those things that dozens of other speakers didn't also have at their fingertips. So instead, I thought I would speak about something that I know intimately, probably the only thing I know well enough to offer any words of wisdom on.

I am a white, Jewish, brown-eyed, Northern, gay, Russian and Polish descent female artist...but of all those things, the only one I lay claim to is being an artist. That's the only thing I can take credit for, because everything else is merely an accident of birth.

One is *born* with talent—that is an accident of birth as well. But one *makes* oneself an artist. And as corny as it sounds, I *believe* in art. I believe that art has the power to heal the broken spirit, to succor the frightened soul. To redeem, not just the listener or the watcher, but the artist, as well. To make sense out of chaos. To hold a mirror up to the world, when the world forgets what it looks like. To issue both a warning and an exaltation.

To be born an artist is to be born an outlaw. I've said that over and over again this week, to looks of understanding on the part of people much younger than myself. And I'm so *grateful* to be able to pass that on, because I think that's one of the most frightening things, when you grow up with talent. You *search* for your kind. You come to Berklee thinking that you will finally find them. And you discover eventually that, if you're lucky, there will be a few people in your lifetime who *really* understand. But by and large, as an artist, you stand alone. And that is both glorious and horrible.

To be born with the possibility of attaining what Nietzsche refers to as "the aristocracy of merit," placing us *above* people who were born to be kings and queen. To be born royal, that's an accident of birth. Whereas I have *sat* with kings and queens, and they have asked for *my* opinion—because I *attained* the aristocracy that my talent entitled me to.

We are dangerous, we artists, because we accept nothing at face value, including our own worth. We question everything. We always start with "Why?", and we end with "Yes, but then,

In *The Republic*, Plato (c.427 B.C.-c.348 B.C.) defines concepts of social and personal justice. He argues that poets encourage people to sympathize with characters who behave unjustly.

why?" We follow all problems to the source; we question all systems; we never stop searching.

It is no accident that Plato calls for the banishment of artists in his perfect society, before he banishes anyone else. We are, by nature, outlaws, as I said, and art, by nature, is seditious. Art accepts no truth but its own. Art insists on being seen and on being heard, whether we want to or not.

Art just *is*. When our trust in politics has run out, when our faith in humanity has run out, art is there to make sense out of chaos.

To be an artist is to simultaneously occupy heaven and hell. We're born with our talent. We can nurture it, we can protect it, we can make it our own, but we cannot take full credit for it, because the talent is a grace. It's a gift.

And the talent we bear is ephemeral. There's not an artist alive who can honestly tell you where their inspiration comes from. Those that do are lying through their teeth. We have no idea. If we knew, every piece of art would be a great piece of art.

But it's ephemeral. And because it's ephemeral, it's frightening.

No singers can guarantee that on this particular night, their voice will be at its best. No players can promise you that they will take their greatest solo on your night. There are too many random elements. There are too many things working against us. Just the physical elements alone: Did I walk too far? Did I walk too fast? Did I rise too early? Did I rise too late? Did I eat too much? Did I not eat enough? All of these things affect us—and our instruments, which misbehave even under the best of circumstances.

And there are also the intangibles. Did I look in the mirror when I changed my clothes, and decide yet again that I hate my body? Am I embarrassed by it when I go on stage? Did I leave too much of my heart at home, when my heart belongs right here, doing the work that I'm meant to do?

All of these things affect us, and because they're so completely out of control, very often we seek to control the world around us instead.

Our biggest fear, of course, is that since the talent is so ephemeral, it will dry up, and it will leave us—alone and naked without its support. Because when you're born with a great talent, you come to rely on that talent to make you special. To hold you at night, when there's no one there. To remind you that you are, in fact, important, when the entire world says to you "That's just silly. Go be a lawyer. Go be a dentist. Go be a doctor. Do something with your life. *Anything*, other than this."

We fear that our talent will leave us naked, without its strength and its protection. And because of that fear, we become jealous guardians of our superstitions, our rules and regulations, and our illusory ability to *control* the world around us. Even I myself, at fifty-nine, having been a professional performer since I was the age of thirteen—even I find myself often saying, "Well, more *me* is always a good thing! Keep feeding *me*. Keep feeding *me*. Keep feeding *me*."

And, if we don't watch it, that heaven turns into hell.

I haven't had a hit record in decades; I refer to myself as "semi-famous." What that means to me is that I get to earn a living doing music. I don't have to take a job at Starbucks. I don't have to have a day job. Being "Janis Ian" *is* my day job. And on a week like this, believe me, it's quite a thorough job.

I'm well-known enough to get enough work to support myself and support myself well, but I'm not so well-known that I need a retinue to stand between me and the world. But I have had platinum records in pretty much every Western country, and I've toured behind all of them, and I remember the fear.

It's hard to be a commodity. And yet the only way to earn a living as an artist is to be a commodity of one sort or another. We sell soap, we artists. We sell soap. There's no way around it, if you want to earn a living. Our only hope is to make our soap just a *bit* better than the next person's soap. To make the audience aware that our soap exists, and then to try and keep our soap as pure as possible.

Odetta Holmes (1930–2008) was an American singer and songwriter, who influenced a number of folk musicians, including Bob Dylan and Joan Baez.

It's easy to become overwhelmed with the amount of people pressing you for decisions and impinging on your time. Odetta told me when I was sixteen, "Always remember, you do not work for *them*. They work for *you*." But a scant few months before she died, my cherished friend told me she had not been able to live up to those words herself. We artists scare too easily.

We are surrounded by people who earn their livings through us. My U.S. booking agents would have me spend all my time on the road, so they can make their commissions. My foreign booking agents can't understand why I don't want to spend a year in Japan or in England. My recording affiliates want me to spend all of my time touring behind my records, when they're released in *their* countries, so that they can sell CDs and make their money back. My co-writers would like me home in Nashville more often, so that we can write more songs. My business managers want me to make as much money as possible as quickly as possible, so I'm safe in my old age, and my partner Pat would just like to *see* me once in a while.

It's easy to become overwhelmed. And when you become overwhelmed, you begin to say "No" to everything, because that's the only control you feel you have. And that being overwhelmed is what leads to the wretched excesses we watch on television and read about in the magazines, every day.

I have toured with a U.S. artist who insists that a barber chair be brought in, so that she can have her makeup done while she sits comfortably in it. It never occurs to her that someone has to haul that chair up four flights of stairs in an old theater. I've watched another American artist show up with fifteen outfits and then demand that someone be found to iron and press them all and hang them neatly on a rack, with the matching shoes in front of each, so that at the last minute, she can decide which one to wear.

I toured in Australia after another American artist, playing all the same venues, visiting the same television stations—and it was appalling how frightened the crew were of *me*, because she had just come through.

That kind of behavior is unconscionable. It's appalling. But we, as artists, and commodities, become surrounded by people in whose best interest it is to keep us as ignorant and as childish as possible. And to cater to those whims, so that if an artist says, "I really don't like people staring at me," suddenly it's in the contract—*No one look at the artist.*

You think I'm *joking*. This is in *contracts*.

The worst example I ever saw—and the most humiliating to me as a representative of artists—was when I toured Ireland with a promoter named Jim Aiken. He was the sort of promoter you could do a handshake deal with and you knew you would get paid fair and square. He came on tour with me and he said, "Oh, my wife is a huge fan—would you sign this for her?" And I said, "Sure, and let me invite her to some shows."

Well, she never came, and I went back two years later and I toured again, and I said, "Is your wife coming?" and he said, "Oh, I don't think so."

It was only in my third tour that he trusted me enough to bring his wife. He brought her backstage at my request, and I politely thanked her for not minding that Jim had spent the last three weeks with me on tour.

I said my goodbyes, and then I said to him, "She's a lovely woman. Why did this take so long?"

He said that the last time he had introduced her to an artist she loved, the artist had been polite, had shaken her hand, and then asked to speak with Jim privately…and had then said in no uncertain terms, "When *I* am on tour with *you*, I am the *only* woman in your life! I do not want to see that woman near me again."

I don't excuse that behavior, but I do seek to explain it and to warn you against it. This woman is extremely famous. This woman is extremely healthy and wealthy and unhappy. And it serves her right, because she's left a legacy of fear behind her. And if there's anything, as artists, that we are responsible for to the community—it is to ease their terror, not to add to it.

I digress….We live in a state of fear as artists. Our booking agents will fire us. Our managers will leave us. There will be nothing left for us. Everyone will desert us, and there will be nothing. It doesn't look like that to people on the outside, but that's what it feels like on the inside. And sometimes, as you heard from these stories, that turns us into monsters.

But concurrent with hell, there is always heaven.

A friend of mine asked me what it was like for me, when I was in the middle of a song or a project. She said, "You are so concentrated in those moments, I do believe the world could fall apart, and you would not notice." And she was right.

The Buddhists speak of "Being in the moment." Well, when you're in that moment of creation, nothing else exists. You are moving so fast, and so slowly at the same time, that you encompass a universe.

I told her, when she asked what it was like, that it was like being on the back of a runaway horse without a saddle or a bridle. As you seek desperately to hang on, hoping you don't fall off before the horse is done with you….And when you're finished, you realize that you've just had the ride of your life.

That's how I put it politely.

If I had been saying it to a close friend, I would have said, "You know what? It beats the best sex you've ever had. *Nothing* comes close."

And *that's* why, as artists, we are so driven. *That's* why we keep going back. For that one singular moment, that puts us on a par with God. That allows us to be creators. That stands us above all of the people out there who will never know that moment, except through our work.

Anyone who lives with a dedicated artist knows that they will never be wife or husband to that artist—they will always be mistress. And as I kept telling my classes, that's all right. It's not unfair. It is in the nature of an artist to take everything offered and to still want more. To question every moment.

There's a classic story about Charles Baudelaire breaking up with his mistress, and he suddenly rose from the bed where they'd been arguing and he ran to the bathroom. He looked in the mirror at his tears, and she said, "What are you doing?!" And he said, "I may need these some day…I want to know what I look like."

Now that's both horrifying and exalting, because you can't use your talent as an excuse for being a jerk. It just doesn't work that way. The world has enough ways to knock you down without you giving them excuses.

As an artist I believe it is my job to make sense of chaos. To speak the unspeakable, to reveal what is hidden. To make sure that *no one forgets history.*

> Charles Baudelaire (1821-1867) was a French poet and essayist of the Romantic era, whose most famous work was *Les Fleurs du mal* (*The Flowers of Evil*).

Particularly the young artists, who think that their history began and ended with the 1960s or the 1970s or the 1980s. Or, if they're educated, maybe with the Greeks. Who don't realize that our history as artists goes back to the very first person living in a cave, who came home from the hunt and drew a picture of that hunt on the walls.

Whatever my lineage is as a Jew, whatever my lineage is as an American, my lineage as an artist stands above all of that. And there comes a point in every artist's life when they must decide: "Will you be a citizen of a country or will you be a citizen of the world?" Because you cannot be *both.*

Artists don't start wars. Artists understand that fighting over a piece of land is absurd. Artists know these things instinctively. Artists don't go into politics. Who would want to embarrass their work that way?

I try to live a life congruent with my vision of what an artist is. I am all too aware that I stand upon the bones of those who went before me. I am all too aware that the higher I stand on those bones, the farther I can see.

And so when I look at my lineage, I try to look at my lineage as an unbroken continuum that began with the first person who *thought* and brings me to this day among people who *think.*

If we allow ourselves and our lives as artists to become corrupted, until we care more for ourselves than we care for our work, then we're no longer standing on that pile of bones. And the work will forget us.

But it's hard, in this increasingly fragmented world, to maintain the energy and the concentration and the openness that are required, in order to be an artist, when there are so many temptations.

We are lucky, though. We in this room are lucky, because we are in the theater. The theatre makes us strong. The theatre is ritual. The theatre is tradition. Visual artists don't have a theater. Musicians have theater, actors have theater, and dancers have theater. We are fortunate.

If we didn't have ritual and tradition, we would fall apart at the seams. Think about the amount of ritual and tradition you go through every day. You pass someone in the street, you nod at him or her, and you smile to show that you're not a threat. You shake hands with your right, to show you're not holding a sword in it. You hold a napkin in your lap, so you don't spill food all over your host's floor. Manners are morals.

These things are all tradition and ritual. The theatre has its own thousands of tiny rituals. We never say "Good luck!" It's tempting the Fates, who may be listening, and they may decide to screw with us and instead break your leg. We say "Break a leg," so that if the Fates are watching, they don't.

We don't whistle backstage, because in the old days that was a signal for the scaffolding to come down, and it would come down on your head.

We are superstitious, and those of us who are not...are.

Theatre is ritual. And ritual is *magic*. The Catholic Church knows that. Costumes. Props. Incense. All of the things you use to give the illusion that you are bigger than most. In theater, we must be bigger than most—why else are we here?

At the end of the day, that's what we artists do. We make magic. We are alchemists of the soul. We turn lead into gold. Sorrow into song. We take *nothing*, thin air, and we beat it into a wedding band. We transmute the ordinary happenstance of life, turning coal into diamonds, emeralds. We make it visible, so that when times get really hard, we can say "Here's a song about your life. Here's a film that shows you who you can be. Here's play, here's a vision, here's a moment to grab hold of and cherish."

Our great strength, and our great privilege, is to hold on to the dreams of those around us. To speak for the silent. To give voice to the voiceless. So that when all hope is gone...when humanity forgets...we are there to remind them.

It's our job to grasp their longing and their yearning, because they can't do it for themselves. It is our job to seize their hopes and dreams, their triumphs and their failures—to grab them in our hands and hold them safe.

That's alchemy at its best. To transform the hopes and fears of a *world*. To hold a mirror up to their eyes, and let them see—not just what they *think* they are—but what they *truly* are, and what they can become.

We offer them redemption through truth.

And that's what it is, in my world, to be an artist in the highest sense. To *serve*. To live in service to your talent, to your work. To the community that supports you. To live in service to your gift. So that for the non-artist, there *is* someone there to bring order out of chaos.

And when the world collides with itself, and all the balls that everyone is juggling up in the air not only come crashing to the ground but beat them about the head.... When life gets *so* hard that people forget they even know *how to* dream...we are there. We are there with the dreams that we have kept safe. We are there to say, "Here are your dreams. You can have them again, because I've held them for you."

That's our job.

We are there with them, from cradle to grave. We sing them into this world, and we sing them out. We are the past, and we are the future. We are the best that humanity has to offer. We are artists, and *that is our job*.

There's a great Zen parable. In Japan, they have the Living Treasure, where if you're considered a great artist whose work and methodology are in danger of dying out, the government says, "You are a Living

Treasure, and we will support you, and in turn, you will teach certain students to carry on your tradition."

Well, there was a young Japanese painter—brush painter—and he was picked to study with a Living Treasure. So he went from his small town to study with this idol, hoping to leap from being a good artist to a great one, with all the wealth and notoriety that entailed. And he walked in the first day and his teacher said, "Draw me a fish."

And so, very quickly, he drew the most beautiful fish...and the teacher, a few minutes later, looked at it, tore it up, and said, "Thank you. Come tomorrow."

The boy went away a little confused, but he thought, "Well, maybe I just didn't draw beautifully enough. I'll do better tomorrow." So the next day, he came to the teacher and said, "Here," handing him a more beautiful drawing of a fish. And the teacher said, "Thank you," tore it up, let the pieces fall to the floor, and said, "Come back tomorrow."

The next day, they went fishing, and the boy caught a fish, and the teacher gave him his own room. There was the fish, beautifully laid out on a stand, and the teacher said, "You will come here every day, and you will draw this fish once."

And so the boy came, every day, to draw the same fish. And every day, at the end of the day, his teacher looked at the drawing, tore it up, let the pieces fall to the floor, and said, "Come back tomorrow."

Well, you can imagine, as artists, what that did to him. He went through all the stages. First he thought he wasn't good enough. Then he thought he was *too* good, and the teacher was too old. Then he thought the teacher was an idiot. Then he thought the teacher really didn't understand *his* art, because the teacher came from a different form.

He went through all the stages, including grief. He beat himself up and beat himself up. He lifted himself up and lifted himself up. The fish began to rot. The flesh fell from the bones. The stench became so overwhelming that the boy had to tie a kerchief around his face just to walk into the room. Then the beetles came, and he watched as they ate the carcass.

And as he watched, he kept trying to draw the fish. And as he kept drawing the fish, the teacher kept coming in and saying, "That's very nice, come tomorrow," as he tore the drawing into pieces and left them on the floor.

He became a bit demoralized. He was outraged at the futility of his effort, but he persisted, because he couldn't imagine facing his family. He persisted through the maggots. He persisted through the beetles, though his own stomach rebelled and his eyes could barely stand to look any more, because they were watering so hard, until one day, months and months later, only the bones remained.

And he walked in that morning so discouraged that he thought of taking his own life. And he looked at these bones, and he began to cry. And as he cried, he looked at the bones through the lenses of his tears, and as he looked, a miracle happened. He began to see the fish from the outside and then from the inside. And he watched as, from the bones, the flesh grew back. And he began to paint from the inside out.

And when he finished, it was not the most beautiful fish anyone had ever seen, but it was the *essence* of a fish. And that day his master walked in and looked at it and said, "I have nothing else to teach you. You are now a master. Go home."

To me, that is what we do. We learn to see from the inside out.

In my entire life as a songwriter, as a writer, I have tried to see the world from the inside out. And yet...and yet, after fifty-odd years as a musician, that story tells it more eloquently than I ever will.

I thank you for your time.

CONCLUSION

Courage, Vision, Worldview—And Magic

"Now, you are an artist. I can teach you no more," the Zen master tells his student, in the parable that Janis Ian recounts. For the young artist had painted the fish "from the inside out—first the bone, then the muscle, and finally, the flesh. The fish came alive under his hands."

To be an artist, he made "sense of the chaos." He did what artists do, says Ian. He put flesh on bone. He made "magic." As Ian explains, to be an artist means to "take nothing, thin air, and turn it into gold."

The artists you have read in this book share Ian's message. Each, in his or her own unique way, explains what it takes to be an artist and offers both encouragement and life lessons. Each makes it clear that artists need to learn not only their art. They need a broad education, one open to all the world has to offer and teach. To be an artist, they explain, it is necessary to understand oneself; to explore and appreciate the ways that different arts relate to each other; to help sustain culture and community; to bring joy to the world; and to tell the truth.

As Victor Wooten explains, to be an artist, one must be honest, and one must be his or her authentic self. Artists are grounded in a strong sense of values and understand their relationship to community, family, and self.

Nona Hendryx believes that art centers life. "Music is always there, always with you, and never lets you down."

For Bill Banfield, artists help us "see who we are, why we are, and what we mean to each other." They "enable us to understand ourselves and our world."

Michael Bearden knows that every artist has to be him or herself. "Be true to yourself," he says. "Be you. Don't try to be anyone else."

Caroline Harvey urges artists to embrace their identity. "Claim your art…Do not let anyone silence you."

Alisa Valdes-Rodriguez reminds artists to be bold and to listen to their inner voice. She says, "My soul told me that I had to…do this thing. I had to write."

Ellen Priest defines art as being able to "capture that tension in our lives between what is physical and tangible and what isn't." Art helps make sense of that "constant back and forth between the physical and the non-physical." Art makes the non-physical come to life and somehow make sense.

China Blue notes that art "is about inquiry, figuring out how the world works." To be an artist means to ask—and try to answer—"the big questions."

For Henry Diltz, being an artist involves observing the world and presenting it back to others. Artists show us ourselves. Artists watch, record, and "catch something" about the world that the rest of us do not see.

Lori Landay reminds us that artists need to "be patient. Trust yourself. Do not be afraid to share your vision."

This trust in oneself leads artists to serve society. As Bruce George explains, art enables people to move beyond themselves, out of the individualistic and towards the social, connecting with each other and working for some larger good. Art is not about the "I," says George. "It is about the *we*."

For Doug Stanton, to be an artist means to try and make sense of the world—to create "a tonality or a narrative in a world that seems to be extremely bifurcated, atonal, and not rhyming in any sense of the word." This requires a comfort with complexity, and a curious and creative mind, one that seeks knowledge and is dedicated to learning.

Otis Sallid extends this theme as he emphasizes that art is a language. To be an artist is to communicate widely, to connect to others by learning and speaking art's "languages."

Artists, says Greg Jaris, help people see the wonder all around us. They "re-enchant the world to its magic."

Bobby McFerrin tells us that art "lifts people up. It not only gets you to tap your feet and move your body. Through the music, the artist gets you to look at yourself in some new way. It is not about looking at the artist so much, but about looking at whatever the artist is showing you that relates to you—your own personality, your own being—that makes you think about your life and what you're doing. It is not just, 'Wow, man, you're really cool. I really like what you do,' but it is, 'I really like what you have done for me or what you do to me.'

"Artists," says McFerrin, "should be in the business of heart surgery, changing people's hearts."

This heart surgery brings the world joy. It is powerful. It can, as Janis Ian tells us, "heal the broken in spirit," "give strength to the fragile," and "ease the weary soul."

The artists we have read recognize the way artists affect and are affected by the world in which we live. The artists featured in this book accept their roles and their responsibilities. They understand that society needs them to tell the truth.

To be an artist, one needs courage, perseverance, and dedication. It is hard work. But it is also wonderful and necessary work.

Art shows us our best and our worst. It helps us understand our past and our present. It enables us to envision our future.

To all artists—for your courage, vision, and worldview; for your tirelessness and for your imagination—thank you. We look forward to the future that you create.

FURTHER READING

Arnheim, Rudolf. *Art and Visual Perception: A Psychology of the Creative Eye*. Berkeley: University of California Press, 2004. Print.

Banfield, William C. *Cultural Codes: Makings of a Black Music Philosophy: An Interpretive History from Spirituals to Hip Hop*. Lanham MD: Scarecrow, 2010. Print.

Banfield, William C. *Musical Landscapes in Color: Conversations with Black American Composers*. Lanham, MD: Scarecrow, 2003. Print.

Elkins, James. *Why Art Cannot Be Taught: A Handbook for Art Students*. Urbana: University of Illinois Press, 2001. Print.

Fawcett, Anthony, and Henry Diltz. *California Rock, California Sound: The Music of Los Angeles and Southern California*. Los Angeles: Reed, 1978. Print.

Ian, Janis. *Society's Child: My Autobiography*. New York: Jeremy P. Tarcher/ Penguin, 2008. Print.

Landay, Lori. *I Love Lucy*. Detroit: Wayne State University Press, 2010. Print.

Landay, Lori. *Madcaps, Screwballs, and Con Women: The Female Trickster in American Culture*. Philadelphia: University of Pennsylvania Press, 1998. Print.

Langer, Susanne K. *Feeling and Form*. Routledge and Kegan Paul, 1967. Print.

Langer, Susanne K. *Philosophy in a New Key: A Study in the Symbolism of Reason, Rite, and Art*. Cambridge: Harvard University Press, 1951. Print.

Mandela, Winnie. Ed. by Anne Benjamin, Adapted by Mary Benson. *Part of My Soul Went with Him*. NY: W.W. Norton, 1985. Print.

Rivera, Louis Reyes, and Bruce George. *The Bandana Republic: A Literary Anthology by Gang Members and Their Affiliates*. Brooklyn, NY: Soft Skull Press, 2008. Print.

Singerman, Howard. *Art Subjects: Making Artists in the American University*. Berkeley: University of California Press, 1999. Print.

192 \ To Be an Artist: Musicians, Visual Artists, Writers, and Dancers Speak

Stanton, Doug. *Horse Soldiers: The Extraordinary Story of a Band of U.S. Soldiers Who Rode to Victory in Afghanistan.* New York: Scribner, 2009. Print.

Stanton, Doug. *In Harm's Way: The Sinking of the USS Indianapolis and the Extraordinary Story of Its Survivors.* New York: Henry Holt, 2001. Print.

Tillich, Paul. *Theology of Culture.* NY: Oxford University Press, 1959. Print.

Wooten, Victor. *The Music Lesson: A Spiritual Search for Growth through Music.* New York: Berkley, 2008. Print.

INDEX

Lauper, Cyndi, 14, 21
Lee, Spike, 41, 140
Leiserowitz, Mel, 156
Leslie, William, 39-40
Letterman, David, 36
Lopez, George, 36, 38, 43, 62
Lopez, Jennifer, 36, 38, 62
The Lovin' Spoonful, 92
Lowell, Amy, 110

Ma, Yo-Yo, 162
Madonna, 25, 27, 36, 38-39
Mailer, Norman, 130
Mandela, Nelson, 19, 20
Mandela, Winnie, 19, 22
Mann, Herbie, 37
Martin, Ricky, 36
Mayfield, Curtis Lee, 10, 18
McCarthy Hearings, 47
McCartney, Paul, 92, 97
McDonnell, Terry, 127, 129
McFerrin, Bobby, xiv, 149, 161-170, 188
McFerrin, Robert Sr., 165
McKnight, Brian, 36
McMillan, Terry, 68
McVeigh, Timothy, 173
Messina, Jim, 97
Midler, Bette, 172
Minnelli, Liza, 36, 39
Mitchell, Joni, 92, 96, 98
Modern Folk Quartet, 92, 95-96
Monk, Thelonious, 176
The Monkees, 92
Monterey Pop Festival, 92

Nash, Graham, 92-93
New Orleans, 64
New York City, 143-145
Nietzsche, Friedrich, 177
Nirvana, 25

Obama, Michelle, 40, 42
Obama, President Barack, 36, 42
Ochs, Phil, 96
Ono, Yoko, 36
OpenSim, 104

Paar, Jack, 43
Parker, Charlie, 63
Pattison, Pat, xi, 177
Picasso, Pablo, 27, 85, 135
Plato's Republic, 178
Poetry Slam, 53-54, 121
Pollock, Jackson, 72, 80, 134
Porgy and Bess, 16
Powell, Adam Clayton, 144
Priest, Ellen, xiv, 59, 71-81, 188
Prince, 27
Pryor, Richard, 92
Puff Daddy, 172

Race Movies, 145
Race, 145-146
Randolph-Wright, Charles, 14, 16
Raynor, Louis Benjamin, 156
Reyes Rivera, Louis, 116, 119
Richard, Keith, 14, 92
Richardson, Bill, 62
Richie, Lionel, 36, 38-39
Rivera, Jerry, 67
Robeson, Paul, 47
Rolling Stone Magazine, 14, 99-100, 129
The Rolling Stones, 14, 17, 25
Ronstadt, Linda, 92
Rosenwinkel, Kurt, 65
Rothko, Mark, 72
Rubin, Rick, 121

Salinger, J.D., 135
Sallid, Otis, xv, 113, 139-147, 188
Scorsese, Martin, 41
Second Life, 104, 109-110
Seeger, Peggy, 95
Seeger, Pete, 95
Sellars, Peter, 47-48, 54
Senegal, 31-32
Sexton, Anne, 54
Simmons, Russell, 116, 121
Simon, Edward, 72-73
Simon, Paul, 96
Simone, 14
SkinDiver, 14,16, 22